STECK-VAUGHN

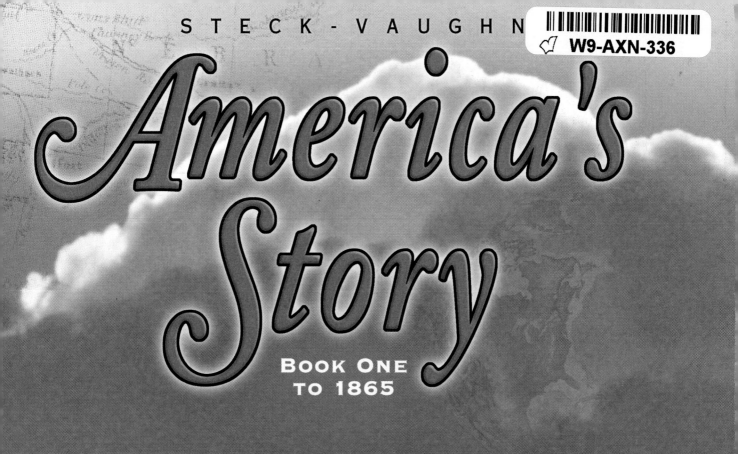

America's Story

BOOK ONE
TO 1865

Vivian Bernstein

STECK-VAUGHN
ELEMENTARY · SECONDARY · ADULT · LIBRARY
A Harcourt Company

www.steck-vaughn.com

ABOUT THE AUTHOR

Vivian Bernstein is the author of *America's History: Land of Liberty, World History and You, World Geography and You, American Government*, and *Decisions for Health*. She received her Master of Arts degree from New York University. Bernstein is active with professional organizations in social studies, education, and reading. She gives presentations to school faculties and professional groups about social studies instruction and improving content area reading. Bernstein was a teacher in the New York City Public School System for a number of years.

ACKNOWLEDGMENTS

Editorial Director: Diane Schnell
Editor: Meredith Edgley O'Reilly
Associate Director of Design: Joyce Spicer
Designers: Ted Krause, Alexandra Corona
Media Researchers: Claudette Landry, Sarah Fraser
Electronic Production Artist: Linda Reed
Electronic Production Specialists: Dina Bahan, Alan Klemp
Production Coordinator: Rebecca Gonzales

CREDITS

Photo Credits: Cover: (American flag) Corbis; (George Washington, Abraham Lincoln, Harriet Tubman, *Mayflower*, Lewis and Clark with Sacagawea, antique map) The Granger Collection; Back Cover: (Elizabeth Cady Stanton, Frederick Douglass, Sequoya, pioneers, steamboat) The Granger Collection; (Constitution) Reagan Bradshaw; p.2 ©North Wind Pictures; pp.4, 5, 6a, 6b ©The Granger Collection; p.9 ©Bettmann/CORBIS; pp.10a, 10b ©The Granger Collection; p.10c ©North Wind Picture Archives; p.14 ©The Granger Collection; p.15a ©Bettmann/CORBIS; pp.15b,16 ©North Wind Picture Archives; p.17 ©Eric Neurath/Stock Boston; pp.20, 21a, 21b, 22, 25, 26, 27a, 27b ©The Granger Collection; p.27c ©Bettmann/CORBIS; pp.28a, 28b, 28c, 28d, 28e ©APVA Jamestown Rediscovery; p.31 ©The Granger Collection; p.32a ©Bettmann/CORBIS; pp.32b, 32c, 33 ©The Granger Collection; p.34 ©North Wind Picture Archives; pp.38, 40, 41a ©The Granger Collection; p.41b ©Uniphoto; p.41c ©North Wind Picture Archives; p.42 ©The Granger Collection; pp.43, 46 ©Bettmann/CORBIS; p.47a ©The Granger Collection; p.47b ©Reagan Bradshaw; p.47c ©The Granger Collection; p.48a ©The Valentine Museum; pp.48b, 48c, 49a ©The Granger Collection; pp.49b, 53 ©Bettmann/CORBIS; pp.54, 55a, 55b ©The Granger Collection; p.58 ©Bettmann/CORBIS; p.59a ©The Granger Collection; p.59b ©Uniphoto; pp.60, 61a ©The Granger Collection; p.61b ©North Wind Picture Archives; p.65 ©The Granger Collection; p.66a ©Reagan Bradshaw; p.66b ©Uniphoto; p.67a ©Reagan Bradshaw; p.67b ©Henryk T. Kaiser/Photri; p.67c ©Uniphoto; p.68a ©Keith Jewel; p.68b ©Bob Daemmrich/Uniphoto; pp.72, 74 ©The Granger Collection; p.75a ©Bettmann/CORBIS; p.75b ©North Wind Picture Archives; p.75c ©The Granger Collection; p.76 ©Courtesy The Missouri Historical Society; pp.77, 80, 81a, 81b ©The Granger Collection; p.82a ©Stock Montage; p.82b ©North Wind Picture Archives; pp.82c, 83, 87 ©The Granger Collection; p.88a ©Archive Photos; p.88b ©North Wind Pictures; p.88c ©Kevin Fleming/CORBIS; p.89a ©North Wind Pictures; pp.89b, 90a, 90b, 93, 94a, 94b ©The Granger Collection; p.95 ©Courtesy The New York Public Library; pp.96a, 96b ©North Wind Picture Archives; pp.97, 101 ©The Granger Collection; p.102a ©Brown Brothers; p.102b ©Mount Holyoke College Art Museum, South Hadley, MA; p.102c ©The Granger Collection; p.103a ©CORBIS; pp.103b, 104a ©Bettmann/CORBIS; p.104b ©The Granger Collection; p.108 ©Courtesy The Bucks County Historical Society, Doylestown, PA; pp.110, 111a ©North Wind Picture Archives; p.111b ©Courtesy University of Texas; p.112a ©Courtesy The Institute for Texan Cultures; p.112b ©Courtesy The Barker Texas History Center, University of Texas, Austin; p.112c ©Courtesy The Institute for Texan Cultures; p.112d ©Quinn Stewart; p.113a ©The Granger Collection; p.113b ©Courtesy The Institute for Texan Cultures; p.113c ©The Granger Collection; p.116 ©Courtesy The Texas State Archives; p.117a ©Bettmann/CORBIS; p.117b ©The Granger Collection; pp.119, 122 ©North Wind Picture Archives; pp.124, 125 ©The Granger Collection; p.126 ©Brown Brothers; p.130 ©Bettmann/CORBIS; p.131 ©The Granger Collection; p.132a ©North Wind Picture Archives; p.132b ©The Granger Collection; p.133a ©Bettmann/CORBIS; pp.133b, 134, 138 ©The Granger Collection; p.139a ©Quinn Stewart; pp.139b, 140a ©The Granger Collection; p.140b ©Courtesy The Sophia Smith Collection, Smith College; p.141a ©Bettmann/CORBIS; p.141b ©The Granger Collection.

Cartography: MapQuest.com, Inc.

ISBN 0-7398-2383-3
Copyright ©2001 Steck-Vaughn Company.

Printed and bound in the United States of America.

1 2 3 4 5 6 7 8 9 TPO 05 04 03 02 01 00

CONTENTS

America's Story tells the story of our country. Our country is the United States of America. This book tells how the United States began. It also tells how the United States changed from a small country to a large country.

Our country's story began with American Indians. Later, people came to America from Europe. Great Britain ruled 13 colonies in America. Time passed, and Americans in the 13 colonies fought and won a war against the British. After the war, the colonies became a free country. This country was called the United States of America. The leaders of the United States wrote new laws. The laws protected the freedom of the people.

At first, the United States had only 13 states. Slowly, more and more states became part of the United States.

As the country grew, problems between the northern and southern states also grew. People in the North and South did not agree about slavery. Some southern states decided to leave the United States. They started a new nation. This led to a long, hard war. After the war, the United States became one nation again.

While you read *America's Story*, you can become a better student if you follow these steps. Start by learning the New Words for each chapter. Study the maps and pictures in each chapter. Then read the chapter carefully. Finally, think carefully as you write your answers for the "Using What You've Learned" pages.

As you read this book, you will learn how different Americans built this country. Read on and learn how people have worked to make our country a land of freedom for more than 200 years.

Vivian Bernstein

THE SETTLERS OF AMERICA

What do you think it was like to go across an ocean hundreds of years ago? You would not see land for many days. No one would come to help you if you lost your way. You might get sick. Rats might eat the food on your ship. Yet hundreds of years ago, brave people took this dangerous trip to come to America.

About 500 years ago, people from Europe started coming to America. People came to America for different reasons. Some came to find gold. Others came because they wanted more freedom. Many people from Europe settled in America. The Pilgrims were one group that came to America. But the people from Europe were not the first to live in America. American Indians had been living in America for thousands of years. American Indians helped the Pilgrims and some other groups of settlers live in America.

How did American Indians live their lives? Who were the people from Europe who explored and settled in America? As you read Unit 1, think about why different groups of people made the dangerous trip to America.

1492
Christopher Columbus reaches America.

1534
Cartier explores the St. Lawrence River for France.

1607
The English start Jamestown, Virginia.

1682
La Salle explores the Mississippi River for France.

1733
The last English colony is started in Georgia.

1763
England wins the French and Indian War.

1400 **1500** **1600** **1700** **1800**

1540
Coronado explores the Southwest for Spain.

1619
African slaves are brought to Jamestown.

1754
The French and Indian War begins.

3

THE FIRST AMERICANS

American Indians of the Northwest went fishing for food.

American Indians were the first people to live in America. Long ago they lived in Asia. It is believed that land once connected Asia and America. People moved across this land to a part of America called Alaska. Over time they settled in many parts of America. Today these people are called American Indians. They also are known as Native Americans.

Thousands of years later, people from other lands began coming to America. About 225 years ago, the name of our country became the United States of America. American Indians lived in our country long before it was called the United States. American Indians were the first Americans.

American Indians in different parts of the United States spoke different languages. They also lived in different kinds of houses. They wore different kinds of clothes. They ate different kinds of food. They believed in different **religions**.

Many American Indians lived in the Northwest of the United States. In the Northwest, there were thick forests. There were many fish in the ocean and rivers. American Indians of the Northwest went fishing to get food. They ate fish every day. They traveled in long canoes made from trees in the forest. They also built houses from trees.

Other American Indians lived in the Southwest. In the Southwest, there was little rain. There were few trees. There were very few fish and animals to eat. American Indians of the Southwest became farmers. They used river water to grow food. They grew corn and beans for food. They also grew **cotton**. They made their clothes from cotton.

In the Midwest of the United States, the land is very flat. We call this flat land the Great Plains. Millions of **buffalo** lived on the Great Plains. Many American Indians lived on the Great Plains. They became buffalo hunters. They used every part of the buffalo that they killed. They ate buffalo meat. They made needles from buffalo bones. They made clothes and tents out of buffalo skins.

In the East of the United States, there were many forests. Animals lived in the forests. Many American Indians lived in these forests. They became hunters. They killed deer and turkeys for food. They also became farmers. They grew corn, pumpkins, and beans for their families.

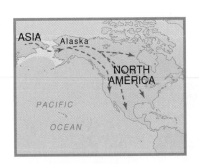

Long ago people walked across land from Asia into America.

Areas of the United States

American Indians who lived on the Great Plains hunted buffalo.

American Indians who lived on the Great Plains made tents out of buffalo skins.

Baskets made by
American Indians
in the East

There were some ways that all American Indians were alike. They loved plants and animals. They took good care of their land. They enjoyed games and telling stories.

All American Indians made their own tools. They needed tools for hunting, farming, and fishing. American Indians made their tools out of stones and animal bones. They made knives out of stones. Some groups of American Indians made metal tools. Many American Indians hunted with bows and arrows. They did not have guns.

American Indians taught many things to people who later came to America. They taught them how to plant foods such as corn, tomatoes, and potatoes. They taught people how to use special plants to make medicines.

There are many American Indians in the United States today. They still enjoy many songs, dances, games, and stories that people enjoyed long ago. But American Indians now work at every kind of job. American Indian medicines are now sold in stores. Many people use them each day. Many people also buy beautiful American Indian art. American Indians today are proud that they were the first people to build our country. They are proud that they were the first Americans.

⭐ Read and Remember

Finish Up   Choose a word in blue print to finish each sentence. Write the word on the correct blank.

Americans	**fishing**	**medicines**
corn	**buffalo**	**hunters**

1. American Indians were the first _____ .

2. American Indians who lived in the Northwest went _____ for their food.

3. American Indian farmers of the Southwest grew beans and

   _____ .

4. Animals that lived on the Great Plains were the _____ .

5. American Indians who lived on the Great Plains became _____ .

6. American Indians used special plants to make _____ .

Think and Apply ⭐

Fact or Opinion   A **fact** is a true statement. An **opinion** is a statement that tells what a person thinks.

> **Fact**   The land is very flat in the Midwest.
> **Opinion**   The Midwest is the best place to live.

Write **F** next to each fact below. Write **O** next to each opinion. You should find two sentences that are opinions.

_____ 1. American Indians spoke different languages.

_____ 2. Millions of buffalo lived on the Great Plains.

_____ 3. It was easy to live on the Great Plains.

_____ 4. American Indians made tools from stones and bones.

_____ 5. The best tools were made from stones.

Skill Builder

Understanding Continents   We live on the planet Earth. Earth has large bodies of land called **continents**. There are seven continents. Most continents have many countries. We live on the continent of North America. Our country, the United States, is in North America.

Here is a list of the continents in order of their size. The largest continent is first on the list.

1. Asia

2. Africa

3. North America

4. South America

5. Antarctica

6. Europe

7. Australia

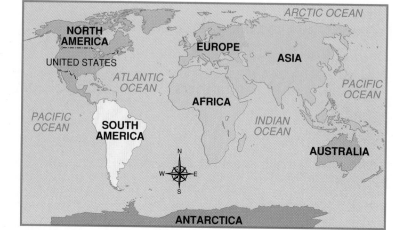

Look at the map above. Write a sentence to answer each question.

1. What are the seven continents? _____

   _____

2. Which continent has the United States? _____

   _____

3. Which is the largest continent? _____

4. Which ocean separates North America from Africa and Europe? _____

   _____

 **Journal Writing**

Think about the different groups of American Indians. Choose two groups. Write about where they lived. Then tell how they got food. Write four to six sentences in your journal.

CHAPTER 2

CHRISTOPHER COLUMBUS

Think About As You Read

1. Which people knew about America before Columbus took his trip?
2. Where did Columbus want to go?
3. Why did Queen Isabella help Columbus?

NEW WORDS

spices
claimed
New World

PEOPLE & PLACES

Christopher Columbus
Italy
Atlantic Ocean
Europe
India
China
Queen Isabella
Spain
Bahamas

After sailing for many days, Christopher Columbus and his crew reached an island in America.

Christopher Columbus lived long ago. Columbus was born in 1451 in Italy. He became a sailor. He also made maps.

In the 1400s, people knew less about the world than we know today. No one knew how large the Atlantic Ocean really was. Some people believed the world was flat. No one in Europe knew there was the land we now call America. Only American Indians knew about their land.

At that time, people from Europe went to India and China to get jewels, silks, and **spices**. India and China are on the continent of Asia. People traveled thousands of miles to the east to reach India and China. Their route was long and dangerous.

Christopher Columbus

Queen Isabella

Christopher Columbus wanted to find an easier way to travel to Asia. Columbus thought the world was round. He believed he could go to India by sailing west across the Atlantic Ocean.

Columbus needed ships and sailors to sail across the Atlantic Ocean. Columbus went to see Isabella, the queen of Spain. Queen Isabella thought about Columbus's plan for seven years. She thought that Columbus might reach India by sailing across the Atlantic Ocean. She wanted Columbus to find gold for Spain. So Queen Isabella decided to help him.

Queen Isabella gave Columbus three small ships. The names of the ships were the *Niña*, the *Pinta*, and the *Santa María*.

Columbus wanted to become rich from his trip. He wanted gold. Queen Isabella said Columbus could keep some of the gold he might find.

Columbus and the sailors sailed west across the Atlantic Ocean for more than a month. They did not see land for

Columbus sailed with three ships—the *Niña*, the *Pinta*, and the *Santa María*.

many days. The sailors were afraid. They wanted to turn back for Spain. But Columbus was brave. He said to sail until October 12. Then they would turn back if they did not see land.

On October 12, 1492, the sailors saw land. On that day the three ships reached a small island.

Columbus thought he was in India. But he was not in India. He was on a small island in the Americas. The island was part of a group of islands. Today these islands are a country called the Bahamas.

People already lived on the island where Columbus landed. Columbus called these people Indians because he thought he was in India. Now they are known as American Indians.

Columbus **claimed** America for Spain. For the people of Europe, America was a **New World**. Of course, it was not a new world to the American Indians who lived there. Soon after Columbus's trip, more people from Europe began to come to America.

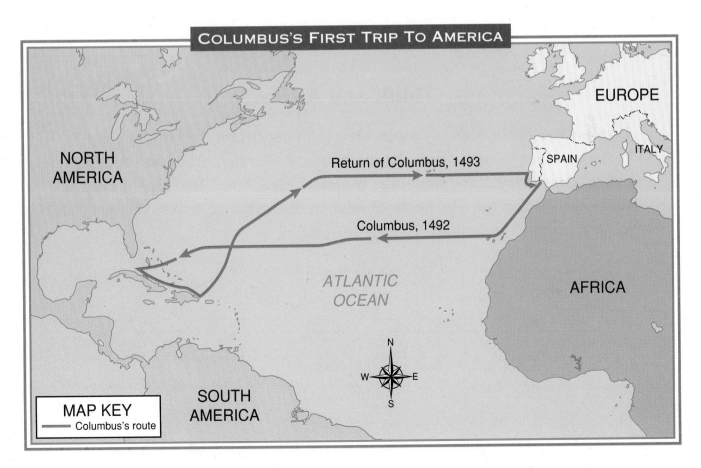

COLUMBUS'S FIRST TRIP TO AMERICA

EUROPE

NORTH AMERICA

SPAIN

ITALY

Return of Columbus, 1493

Columbus, 1492

ATLANTIC OCEAN

AFRICA

N
W   E
S

SOUTH AMERICA

MAP KEY
— Columbus's route

Read and Remember

Choose the Answer   Draw a circle around the correct answer.

1. Where did Columbus want to go?
   America   India   Europe

2. Why did people from Europe want to go to India and China?
   to travel   to get jewels, silks, and spices   to see buffalo

3. What did Queen Isabella give to Columbus?
   jewels   ships   spices

4. What ocean did Columbus sail across?
   Pacific Ocean   Indian Ocean   Atlantic Ocean

5. When did Columbus reach America?
   1412   1451   1492

6. Where did Columbus first land in America?
   in a desert   on the Great Plains   on an island

7. What did Columbus call the people he found in America?
   Indians   Americans   Asians

Think and Apply

Finding the Main Idea   A **main idea** is an important idea in the chapter. Less important ideas support the main idea. Read each group of sentences below. One of the three sentences is a main idea. The other two sentences support the main idea. Write an **M** next to the sentence that is the main idea in each group. The first one is done for you.

1. _____ People wanted jewels from India and China.

   _____ People wanted spices from India and China.

   __M__ People traveled to India and China to get jewels and spices.

2. _____ The route to Asia was dangerous.

   _____ Columbus wanted to find a better route to Asia.

   _____ The route to Asia was very long.

3. _____ In 1492 Columbus and the sailors sailed for many days to reach America.

_____ The sailors did not see land for more than a month.

_____ Columbus had three ships—the *Niña*, the *Pinta*, and the *Santa María*.

4. _____ Columbus sailed west because he wanted to reach India.

_____ No one in Europe knew about America.

_____ When Columbus landed in America, he thought he was in India.

Skill Builder

Using Map Directions The four main directions are **north, south, east,** and **west**. On maps, these directions are shown by a **compass rose**. You can also use the letters **N, S, E,** and **W** to show directions on a compass rose.

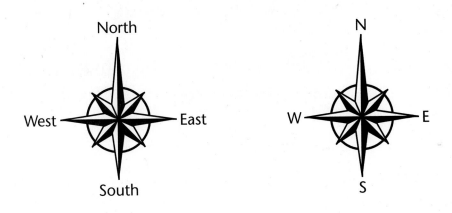

Look back at the map on page 11. Then finish each sentence with the word north, south, east, or **west.**

1. Europe is _____ of the Atlantic Ocean.

2. North America is _____ of the Atlantic Ocean.

3. South America is _____ of North America.

4. Europe is _____ of Africa.

5. Africa is _____ of South America and North America.

6. Spain is _____ of Italy.

CHAPTER 3

THE SPANISH EXPLORE AMERICA

Think About As You Read

1. **Why did the Spanish explore America?**
2. **What did American Indians and the Spanish learn from one another?**
3. **Why did the Spanish build missions?**

NEW WORDS

slavery
missions
priests

PEOPLE & PLACES

Mexico
South America
Spanish
Estevanico
African
Francisco Coronado
Hernando de Soto
Florida
Mississippi River
Southeast
Africa
Catholics
Texas
California
New Mexico
Santa Fe

Estevanico explored the Southwest to find the seven cities of gold for Spain.

Christopher Columbus claimed America for Spain in 1492. People from Spain began to travel across the Atlantic Ocean. They settled in Mexico and South America.

The Spanish heard stories about seven cities that were made of gold. The Spanish wanted to find the cities. They began to explore the land north of Mexico. Today this area is the Southwest of the United States.

The first person to explore the Southwest for Spain was Estevanico. He was an African. In 1539 he searched the Southwest for the seven cities of gold. He never found gold. He was killed by American Indians.

Francisco Coronado

Hernando de Soto

Francisco Coronado also wanted to find the cities of gold. In 1540 he and 300 Spanish soldiers went to the Southwest. Coronado searched for two years. He found American Indian farmers and villages in the Southwest. But he never found the seven cities of gold. In 1542 Coronado went home to Mexico. The king of Spain said the Southwest belonged to Spain.

Hernando de Soto also wanted to find the seven cities of gold for Spain. De Soto started in Florida with more than 700 people in 1539. While he was looking for gold, he came to a very wide river. It was the Mississippi River. He was the first person from Europe to see this river. De Soto never found the seven cities of gold. The Spanish king said that the Southeast area De Soto explored belonged to Spain, too.

American Indians and the Spanish learned from one another. American Indians taught the Spanish to grow American plants. They taught the Spanish to grow beans, tomatoes, corn, pumpkins, and cotton. American Indians taught the Spanish to raise turkeys for food. The Spanish

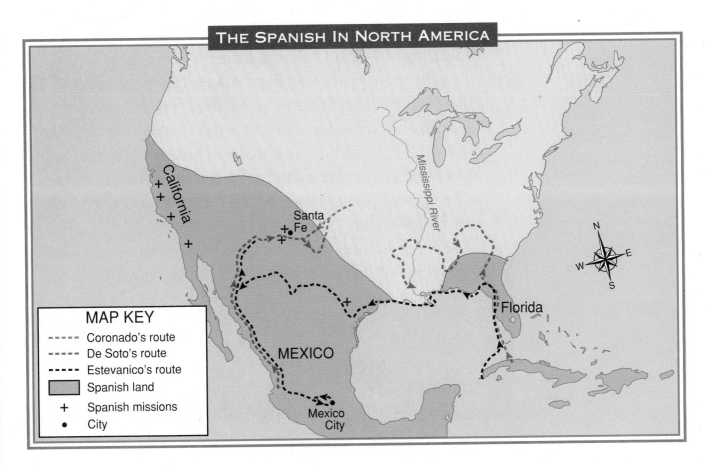

THE SPANISH IN NORTH AMERICA

MAP KEY
- - - - - Coronado's route
- - - - - De Soto's route
- - - - - Estevanico's route
Spanish land
+ Spanish missions
• City

California

Santa Fe

Mississippi River

Florida

MEXICO

Mexico City

N E S W

The Spanish built many missions in America to teach people how to be Catholics.

brought animals from Europe. They brought pigs, cows, sheep, and horses. The Spanish taught the American Indians to grow oranges and wheat.

The Spanish started **slavery** in America. They forced American Indians to be slaves. In 1503 the Spanish started bringing people from Africa to work as slaves. Each year thousands of Africans became slaves in America.

Many Spanish people came to America to find gold. Other Spanish people came to teach American Indians how to be Catholics, people who follow the Catholic religion. That is why the Spanish built **missions** in Texas, California, and New Mexico. Every mission had a church. **Priests** worked in the missions. Priests taught the American Indians to take care of cows, pigs, and sheep.

Sometimes American Indians left the missions because they were not happy. They did not like living with the Spanish. They did not want to follow the Catholic religion. Some missions closed when too many American Indians left.

Other missions became very large. These missions became towns. There was an important Spanish mission in Santa Fe, New Mexico. It helped bring people to Santa Fe. Today Santa Fe is a city. For 300 years the Southwest and Florida belonged to Spain.

Place: Santa Fe, New Mexico

Geographers use five **themes**, or main ideas, to learn about different areas and people on Earth. The theme of **place** tells what makes an area different from other areas in the world. Place tells about an area's land, plants, and weather. It also tells about an area's people and what they built there.

Read the paragraphs about Santa Fe. Study the photo and the map.

Santa Fe is the **capital** of New Mexico. It is in the Southwest of the United States. The Spanish built it around 1610. Santa Fe is in high hills near the Sangre de Cristo Mountains. It is the highest and oldest capital in the nation. It has many buildings made from bricks of dried mud.

Many Pueblo Indians live in villages around Santa Fe. Pueblo Indians lived in the Santa Fe area long before the Spanish came. In 1610 the Spanish built a mission in Santa Fe for American Indians. Today it is called the San Miguel Mission.

On a separate sheet of paper, write the answer to each question.

1. In what area of the United States is Santa Fe, New Mexico?
2. What mountains are near Santa Fe?
3. What are many buildings in Santa Fe made of?
4. Who live in villages around Santa Fe?
5. Look at the map. What river goes through Santa Fe?
6. What are two buildings that people built in Santa Fe?

⭐ Read and Remember

Finish the Sentence   Draw a circle around the word or words that finish each sentence.

1. The first person to explore the Southwest for Spain was _____ .
   Estevanico   Columbus   De Soto

2. Coronado explored the _____ of the United States.
   Northwest   Southwest   Southeast

3. De Soto looked for gold in _____ .
   Florida   New Mexico   California

4. De Soto was the first person from Europe to see the _____ .
   Atlantic Ocean   Northeast   Mississippi River

5. Estevanico, Coronado, and De Soto tried to find the _____ cities of gold.
   five   six   seven

6. The Spanish built _____ for the American Indians.
   farms   stores   missions

Think and Apply ⭐

Categories   Read the words in each group. Decide how they are alike. Choose the best title in blue print for each group. Write the title on the line above each group. The first one is done for you.

Hernando de Soto   **King of Spain**
Francisco Coronado   **Explorers**

Francisco Coronado

1. looked for seven cities of gold
   explored the Southwest
   found American Indian villages

2. said the Southwest belonged to Spain
   said the Southeast belonged to Spain
   ruler of Spain

____

3. Estevanico
   Francisco Coronado
   Hernando de Soto

____

4. looked for seven cities of gold
   explored Florida
   saw the Mississippi River

Skill Builder

Using a Map Key Maps often show many things. Sometimes a map uses little drawings to show what something on the map means. A **map key** tells what those drawings mean. Look at the map key below. On the correct blanks, write what each drawing means.

MAP KEY	
-----	Coronado's route
-----	De Soto's route
-----	Estevanico's route
▭	Spanish land
+	Spanish missions
•	City

+ 1. ______________________

• 2. ______________________

▭ 3. ______________________

----- 4. ______________________

Use the map and map key on page 15 to finish these sentences. Circle the number or word that finishes each sentence.

1. There are ______ missions on this map.
   20 10 7

2. There were ______ missions in California.
   4 10 15

3. The ______ River is on this map.
   Mississippi Florida Santa Fe

4. De Soto's route began in the ______.
   east north west

5. Coronado's route began in the ______.
   north south east

THE PILGRIMS' THANKSGIVING

CHAPTER 4

Think About As You Read

1. Why did the Pilgrims want to go to America?
2. What happened to the Pilgrims during their first winter in America?
3. How did American Indians help the Pilgrims?

NEW WORDS

Church of England
freedom of religion
Mayflower Compact
governor
peace treaty

PEOPLE & PLACES

Pilgrims
England
Holland
Dutch
English
Massachusetts
Plymouth
Wampanoag
Massasoit
Squanto

The Pilgrims' trip to America took 65 days. They landed in Massachusetts in November 1620.

A long time ago, the Pilgrims lived in England. All the people in England had to pray in the king's church. This church was called the **Church of England**. The Pilgrims did not like the Church of England. They wanted to pray in their own church.

The Pilgrims left England and went to a small country called Holland. There was **freedom of religion** in Holland. The Pilgrims prayed in their own church in Holland.

The people of Holland are called the Dutch. They speak the Dutch language. The Pilgrims did not like living in Holland. They wanted to keep their English ways. They decided to go to America. In America they could live as they wanted and have freedom of religion.

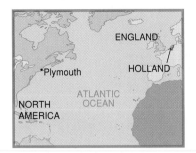

The Pilgrims traveled across the Atlantic Ocean.

In 1620 the Pilgrims left Holland for America. They had a ship. Their ship was the *Mayflower*. The trip took 65 days. The weather was rainy and cold. Many Pilgrims became sick during the long, cold trip.

At last the *Mayflower* reached America. It landed in Massachusetts. Before leaving their ship, the Pilgrims made a plan for a government. That plan was the **Mayflower Compact**. The plan said the Pilgrims would work together to make laws. The laws would be fair to all. The Pilgrims would not have a king in America. They would choose a **governor** and rule themselves. The Mayflower Compact was the first government in America that allowed people from Europe to rule themselves.

The Pilgrims landed in November. They started a town called Plymouth. Plymouth was the second English town in America. In Chapter 5, you will read about the first English town in America.

The first winter in Plymouth was very cold. There was little food. Many Pilgrims became sick and died.

The *Mayflower*

Squanto taught the Pilgrims how to plant corn.

There were no American Indians in Plymouth when the Pilgrims landed. But the Wampanoag were a group of American Indians who lived in forests near Plymouth. They came and helped the Pilgrims. Their leader was Massasoit. He signed a **peace treaty** with the Pilgrims. The Pilgrims and the Wampanoag lived together in peace.

Squanto was an American Indian who taught the Pilgrims how to plant corn. He showed the Pilgrims where to find many fish. He taught the Pilgrims to hunt for deer and turkeys in the forests.

The Pilgrims worked hard in Plymouth. They planted seeds to grow food. They built a church. They built houses. By November 1621 the Pilgrims had a lot of food.

The Pilgrims had a Thanksgiving party in November 1621. They invited their American Indian friends. The American Indians brought deer to the party. The Pilgrims brought turkeys. This Thanksgiving party lasted three days. The Pilgrims gave thanks to God for helping them. They said "thank you" to the American Indians for helping them. This was the Pilgrims' first Thanksgiving in America.

The Pilgrims and the American Indians enjoyed a Thanksgiving party in 1621.

Read and Remember

Choose the Answer   Draw a circle around the correct answer.

1. Where did the Pilgrims first live?
   Holland   England   America

2. What was the name of the Pilgrims' ship?
   Niña   *Mayflower*   *Pinta*

3. Why did the Pilgrims come to America?
   to farm   to have freedom of religion   to meet American Indians

4. What town in America did the Pilgrims start?
   Massachusetts   Plymouth   Santa Fe

Think and Apply

Cause and Effect   A **cause** is something that makes something else happen. What happens is called the **effect**.

Cause   The Pilgrims wanted fair laws
Effect   so they wrote the Mayflower Compact.

Match each cause on the left with an effect on the right. Write the letter of the effect on the correct blank. The first one is done for you.

Cause

1. The Pilgrims did not want to pray in the Church of England, so ___d___

2. The Pilgrims could not keep their English ways in Holland, so _____

3. The Pilgrims had little food for their first winter, so _____

4. The Wampanoag wanted peace, so _____

5. The Pilgrims had a lot of food for their second winter, so _____

Effect

a. many Pilgrims died.

b. Massasoit signed a peace treaty with the Pilgrims.

c. they had a Thanksgiving party to thank God and the American Indians.

d. they went to Holland.

e. they went to America.

Skill Builder

Reading a Flow Chart   A **flow chart** is a chart that shows you facts in their correct order. The flow chart on this page shows how the Wampanoag grew corn in fields in the 1600s. Whole kernels are the seeds of the corn plant. A hoe is a tool for digging in soil.

Read the flow chart. Then circle the word or words that finish each sentence below.

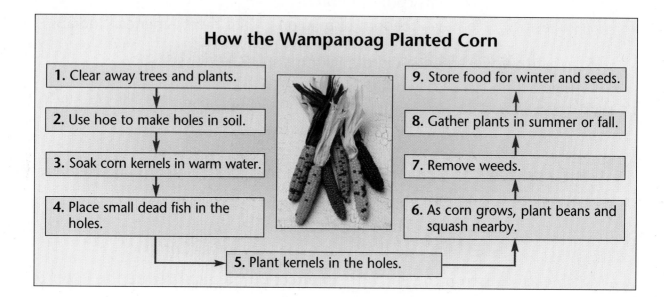

How the Wampanoag Planted Corn

1. Clear away trees and plants.
2. Use hoe to make holes in soil.
3. Soak corn kernels in warm water.
4. Place small dead fish in the holes.
5. Plant kernels in the holes.
6. As corn grows, plant beans and squash nearby.
7. Remove weeds.
8. Gather plants in summer or fall.
9. Store food for winter and seeds.

1. The first step is to _____ trees.
   shake   clear away   plant

2. The American Indians placed _____ with the kernels in the holes.
   fish   worms   weeds

3. In Step 6 beans and _____ are planted nearby.
   squash   tomatoes   orange trees

4. The last step is to _____ some food.
   store   grow   burn

 # Journal Writing

Write a paragraph in your journal that tells why the Pilgrims gave thanks. Give at least three reasons why they might have been thankful.

CHAPTER 5

THE ENGLISH SETTLE AMERICA

Think About As You Read

1. Why was the first winter in Jamestown very hard?
2. Which people came to America for freedom of religion?
3. Why did Roger Williams start Providence?

NEW WORDS

colony
settlers
tobacco
religious
in debt

PEOPLE & PLACES

Jamestown
Virginia
Puritans
Roger Williams
Providence
Rhode Island
Anne Hutchinson
Maryland
New York
Quakers
William Penn
Pennsylvania
James Oglethorpe
Georgia

In 1607 the English started Jamestown in Virginia.

The Pilgrims were not the first group of English people to live in America. The first group of English people came to America in 1585, but their **colony** failed.

Before long more English people moved to America. They came for three reasons. Many people came to get rich. Some people came for freedom of religion. Others came because they thought they could have a better life in America.

In 1607 the English started their first town in America. It was called Jamestown. It was in the Virginia colony. The English came to Jamestown to find gold. They did not find gold.

At first the Jamestown **settlers** did not want to grow food or build houses. The settlers were very hungry during the first winter. Many settlers died. More people came to live in Jamestown. Then the settlers began to work harder. They built farms and houses.

In 1619 the Jamestown settlers brought slaves from Africa to help them grow tobacco.

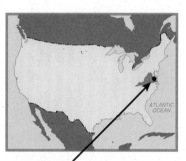

Jamestown, Virginia

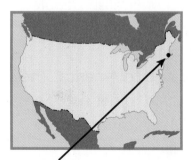

Providence, Rhode Island

The settlers began to grow **tobacco** in Jamestown. People smoked tobacco in pipes. The settlers sold their tobacco to England for a lot of money. Each year the settlers grew more and more tobacco. In 1619 the settlers brought slaves from Africa to help them grow tobacco. After that more African slaves were brought to the English colonies.

The Puritans were a group of people who did not want to pray in the Church of England. In 1628 a group of Puritans came to Massachusetts for freedom of religion. Later, more Puritans came. The Puritans started the first schools in America. Everyone in Massachusetts had to pray in Puritan churches. The Puritans did not let other people have freedom of religion.

Roger Williams lived with the Puritans. He told them that everyone should have freedom of religion. He left Massachusetts and traveled through the forests. Roger Williams met American Indians who helped him. He bought land from them. Roger Williams started the city of Providence on that land in 1636. Later, the land became the colony of Rhode Island. Providence was the first city in America where there was freedom of religion for all.

Anne Hutchinson was a woman who lived in Massachusetts. Her **religious** ideas were different from the Puritan ideas. Anne Hutchinson also left Massachusetts. She went to Rhode Island in 1638 and started a new town.

More English people came to America for freedom of religion. Catholics were sent to jail if they prayed in Catholic churches in England. So 300 Catholics came to America in 1634. They started a colony called Maryland.

People from Holland had started a colony near the Atlantic Ocean in 1624. Then in 1664 England took control of the Dutch colony. It became an English colony. It was called New York.

The Quakers were another group of people who would not pray in the Church of England. William Penn was a Quaker. In 1681 the English king gave Penn some land in America. Penn started the Pennsylvania colony on that land. But Penn also bought the land from American Indians who lived there. The American Indians liked William Penn. There was peace in Pennsylvania. People had freedom of religion in Pennsylvania.

In England there were some people who did not have any money. People who were **in debt** were put into jail. These people could not work or help their families. James Oglethorpe started the Georgia colony to help these people. In 1733 Oglethorpe went to Georgia with 120 of these people. They built homes and farms in Georgia. Poor people from many countries in Europe also moved to the Georgia colony.

Each year more people came to live in the English colonies along the Atlantic Ocean. By 1753 there were 13 English colonies along the Atlantic Ocean.

William Penn

James Oglethorpe

Anne Hutchinson's ideas were different from the ideas of other Puritans.

USING PRIMARY SOURCES

Primary sources are the words and objects of people who have lived at different times. Some primary sources are journals, newspapers, and tools. These words and objects help us learn about people's lives and about history.

We know what life was like in Jamestown from objects that were found there. Parts of beds, curtains, and cooking pots teach us how the settlers lived. Helmets give us clues about how the settlers protected themselves. People have found knives for cutting in Jamestown. They also have found tools for building houses.

The objects on this page were found in the earth at Jamestown. They are from the 1600s. These objects help us understand how Jamestown settlers lived almost 400 years ago.

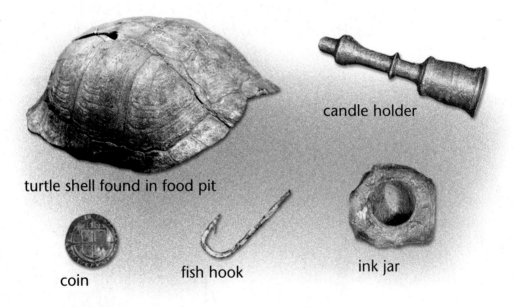

turtle shell found in food pit

candle holder

coin

fish hook

ink jar

On a separate sheet of paper, write the answer to each question.
1. How do we know the Jamestown settlers used money?
2. What object shows that some settlers could read and write?
3. What do you think the settlers did with candles?
4. What are two foods that the settlers probably ate?
5. What is one way that the settlers got food?

USING WHAT YOU'VE LEARNED

★ Read and Remember

Write the Answer   Write a sentence to answer each question.

1. What were three reasons English people came to America? _____

_____

_____

2. Why were African slaves brought to Jamestown? _____

_____

3. Why did the Puritans come to America? _____

_____

4. Which was the first city in America to allow freedom of religion for all? _____

_____

5. Who did James Oglethorpe bring to Georgia? _____

_____

Think and Apply ★

Sequencing Events   Write the numbers **1, 2, 3, 4,** and **5** next to these
sentences to show the correct order. The first one is done for you.

_____   The English started Jamestown, their first town in America.

_____   Roger Williams and Anne Hutchinson left Massachusetts to have
        freedom of religion.

___1___   The first English colony in America failed.

_____   In 1681 William Penn started the peaceful colony of Pennsylvania.

_____   The Puritans started a colony in Massachusetts in 1628.

★ Journal Writing

Which colony would you want to live in if you had moved to America in 1755?
Write a paragraph in your journal that tells which colony you would choose.
Explain your reasons.

Skill Builder

Reading a Historical Map   A **historical map** shows how an area used to look. The historical map on this page shows the 13 English colonies in the year 1753. The 13 colonies are numbered on the map in the order that people from Europe first settled there. Study the map.

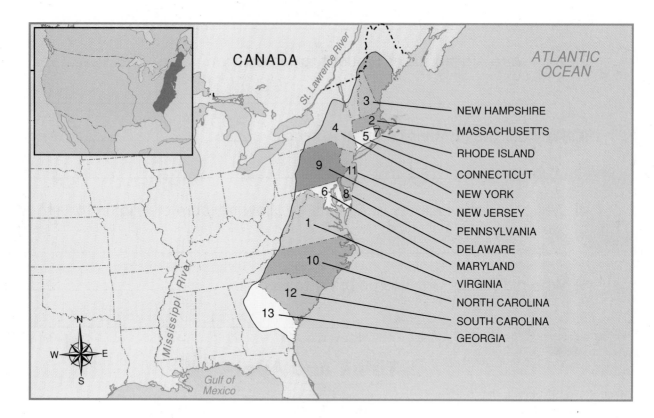

Draw a circle around each correct answer.

1. Which colony was started first?
   Rhode Island   Virginia   Delaware

2. Which colony was started last?
   Georgia   New York   South Carolina

3. Which colony is north of Massachusetts?
   North Carolina   New Hampshire   Maryland

4. Which colony is west of New Jersey?
   Connecticut   Massachusetts   Pennsylvania

THE FRENCH COME TO AMERICA

Think About As You Read

1. Why did the French come to America?
2. How did American Indians help the French?
3. How did France lose most of its land in America?

NEW WORDS

short cut
body of water
snowshoes

PEOPLE & PLACES

France
French
King Louis
Jacques Cartier
Canada
St. Lawrence River
New France
Sieur de la Salle
Gulf of Mexico
Louisiana
St. Louis
New Orleans
George Washington
North America

Jacques Cartier explored the St. Lawrence River for France.

Many English people came to America for freedom of religion. Many poor people came to America to earn money. We learned that many Spanish people came to America to find gold. People from France also came to America. People from France are called the French.

King Louis of France wanted to find a **short cut** to Asia. In 1534 the king sent Jacques Cartier to America. Cartier wanted to find a river in America that he could follow west all the way to Asia. Cartier sailed to Canada. He could not find a river that went to Asia. He explored the St. Lawrence River. Look at the map on page 33. Find the St. Lawrence River. Cartier said that all the land around the St. Lawrence River belonged to France. French land in America was called New France.

La Salle called the land around the Mississippi River "Louisiana."

Sieur de la Salle

Jacques Cartier

Sieur de la Salle also explored America for France. In 1682 La Salle traveled from the St. Lawrence River to the Mississippi River. Then he paddled a canoe down the Mississippi River to the south. In the south there is a **body of water** called the Gulf of Mexico. La Salle was the first person we know of who traveled all the way down the Mississippi River to the Gulf of Mexico.

Sieur de la Salle called the land near the Mississippi River "Louisiana." He put a big cross and a French flag on the land of Louisiana. La Salle said that Louisiana belonged to King Louis of France. The land around the Mississippi River and the land around the St. Lawrence River were part of New France.

The French started two cities on the Mississippi River. These two French cities were St. Louis and New Orleans. New Orleans was near the Gulf of Mexico.

Some French people moved to America. They came for two reasons. One reason was to get furs. American Indians hunted animals for their furs. The French traded with the American Indians for these furs. In France they sold these furs for a lot of money. The second reason the French came was to teach American Indians how to be Catholics.

The French owned much more land in America than the English owned. But there were many more English settlers than French settlers. Few French people wanted to live in America. The French did not allow freedom of religion. Only Catholics could live in New France. So the French colony grew very slowly.

American Indians helped the French in many ways. They taught the French how to trap animals for furs. They taught the French how to use canoes to travel on rivers. They also showed the French how to make **snowshoes**. Many parts of New France had lots of snow in the winter. When the French wore snowshoes, they could walk on very deep snow.

American Indians had fewer fights with the French than with the Spanish or the English. The Spanish had forced American Indians to work as slaves. The French never treated them as slaves. The English took land away from the American Indians in order to build farms and towns. The French did not take American Indian lands.

French fur trapper wearing snowshoes

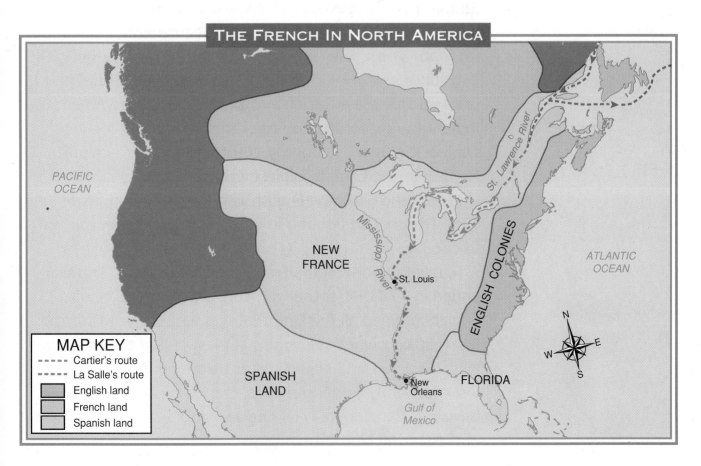

THE FRENCH IN NORTH AMERICA

PACIFIC OCEAN

NEW FRANCE

St. Louis

Mississippi River

St. Lawrence River

ENGLISH COLONIES

ATLANTIC OCEAN

SPANISH LAND

New Orleans

FLORIDA

Gulf of Mexico

MAP KEY
- - - - - Cartier's route
- - - - - La Salle's route
English land
French land
Spanish land

N
W E
S

In 1763 France lost most of its land in America when England won the French and Indian War.

England did not want France to own land in America. Many English people in the 13 colonies wanted to move west to Louisiana. France did not want English people to live in Louisiana. England and France had been enemies in Europe for many years. They became enemies in America. By 1754 England and France were fighting a war in America. This war was called the French and Indian War. Some American Indians fought for the French, and some fought for the English. George Washington lived in the Virginia colony. He helped the English soldiers fight.

The French and the English also fought in Europe. In 1756 they began fighting in Europe. England won this war in 1763.

England also won the French and Indian War. This war ended in 1763. After the war, England owned Canada. England owned all the land that was east of the Mississippi River. Spain owned the land that was west of the Mississippi River. St. Louis and New Orleans belonged to Spain. France lost most of its land in America. France kept two small islands in Canada. In 1763 England and Spain owned most of the land in North America.

⭐ Read and Remember

Finish the Story   Use the words in blue print to finish the story. Write the words you choose on the correct blanks.

furs   Louisiana   Mississippi   canoes   Catholic   French

The French explorer La Salle traveled down the _____

River. He paddled all the way to the Gulf of Mexico. La Salle called all the land

around the Mississippi River "_____ ." This land became part of

the large French colony called New France. Some French people came to America

to get _____ . Others came to teach the _____

religion to American Indians. American Indians taught the French how to use

_____ and snowshoes. In 1763 the _____ lost

the French and Indian War to the English.

Think and Apply ⭐

Fact or Opinion   Write **F** next to each fact below. Write **O** next to each opinion. You should find four sentences that are opinions.

_____ 1. The French king wanted to find a short cut to Asia.

_____ 2. Jacques Cartier explored the St. Lawrence River.

_____ 3. La Salle was a smarter explorer than Cartier was.

_____ 4. The land around the Mississippi and St. Lawrence rivers was part of New France.

_____ 5. Before 1754 France owned more land in America than England did.

_____ 6. Only Catholics could live in New France.

_____ 7. Wearing snowshoes is the best way to walk on deep snow.

_____ 8. New France was a better place to live than the English colonies were.

_____ 9. The French were stronger soldiers than the English soldiers were.

_____ 10. The French and the English fought in Europe and in America.

Skill Builder

Using Map Directions In Chapter 2 you learned that there are four main directions on a map. They are north, south, east, and west. A compass rose also shows four in-between directions. They are **northeast**, **southeast**, **northwest**, and **southwest**. Southeast is between south and east. Southwest is between south and west. Sometimes the in-between directions are shortened to **NE**, **SE**, **NW**, and **SW**.

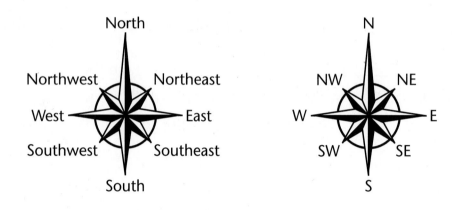

Look at the map on page 33. Then circle the word that finishes each sentence.

1. The St. Lawrence River is in the _____ .
   northeast   northwest   southwest

2. The English colonies were in the _____ .
   northwest   southwest   east

3. The Mississippi River was _____ of the English colonies.
   south   west   east

4. Florida is in the _____ .
   southeast   northeast   northwest

5. The Atlantic Ocean was to the _____ of the English colonies.
   north   west   east

6. New Orleans is in the _____ .
   northwest   northeast   south

UNIT 1 REVIEW

The historical map on this page shows the Spanish, French, and English colonies in North America in 1754. Study the map. Then use the words in blue print to finish the story.

Atlantic Ocean **Gulf of Mexico** **New Orleans** **Florida**
Southwest **St. Lawrence** **Jamestown** **New France**

Spain had land in the Southeast called _____ . Spain also had land in the _____ . Then in 1607 the English started _____ in the Virginia colony. All of the 13 English colonies were near the _____ .

In 1534 Cartier explored a river in Canada called the _____ River. La Salle traveled south on the Mississippi River to the _____ . The French built the city of _____ near the Gulf of Mexico. The French called their colony in America _____ .

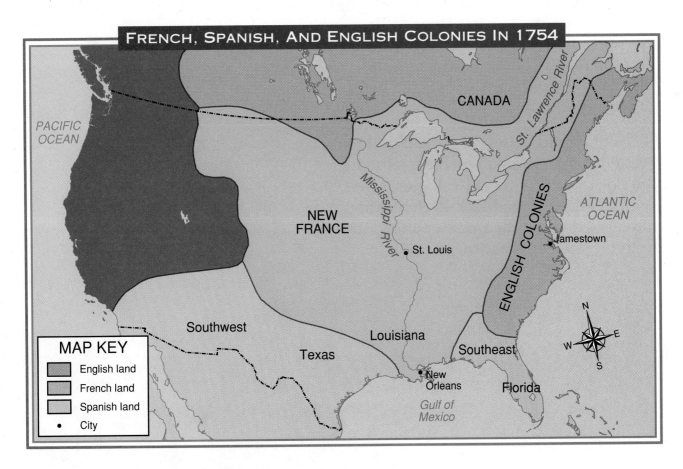

FRENCH, SPANISH, AND ENGLISH COLONIES IN 1754

MAP KEY
- English land
- French land
- Spanish land
- • City

UNIT 2

BUILDING A NEW COUNTRY

Imagine what it was like to live in America in 1776. Many Americans were angry at the British leaders who ruled over them. They were angry about unfair laws that the British leaders wrote for the colonies. Americans became so angry about these laws that they decided to fight for their freedom.

Americans in the 13 colonies were not ready to fight. They did not have enough guns, money, or soldiers. The British army was much stronger. How could the Americans win? It would take the help of many different people, including George Washington.

What would you have done if you had lived in 1776? Would you have joined the fight to make the 13 colonies a free country? As you read Unit 2, think about how Americans built a new country, the United States of America.

1773
Americans throw tea into the Atlantic Ocean at the Boston Tea Party.

1776
Americans write and sign the Declaration of Independence.

1783
Great Britain and America sign a peace treaty.

1789
George Washington becomes the first President of the United States.

1799
George Washington dies.

1760

1770

1780

1790

1800

1765
The British write the Stamp Act.

1775
The American Revolution begins.

1781
Americans win the American Revolution.

1787
Americans write the Constitution.

1791
Americans write the Bill of Rights.

1797
George Washington finishes his work as President.

AMERICANS FIGHT FOR FREEDOM

Think About As You Read

1. Why did Americans think that the new laws from Great Britain were unfair?
2. What happened during the Boston Tea Party?
3. Why did Americans start to fight against the British in 1775?

NEW WORDS

nation
tax
Stamp Act
Parliament
port
Boston Tea Party
American Revolution

PEOPLE & PLACES

Great Britain
British
King George III
Boston

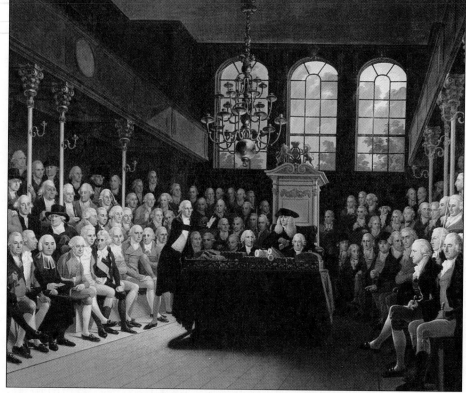

British leaders who made laws were called Parliament.

Many people from England came to live in America. They came to live in the 13 colonies. The people who lived in the colonies were called Americans. Many people came to America because they wanted more freedom.

In 1707 England and three small countries became part of a larger **nation**. The larger nation was called Great Britain. People who lived in Great Britain were called the British. Great Britain ruled the 13 American colonies. The king of Great Britain was the king of the American colonies. From 1760 to 1820, King George III was the king of Great Britain.

In 1763 the English, or British, won the French and Indian War. The war helped the American colonies. Americans felt safer because France no longer ruled Canada. Great Britain ruled Canada after this war. The British had spent a lot of money to fight the French. The British wanted the colonies to help pay for the French and Indian War.

The British made new laws. The laws said that Americans had to send some of their money to Great Britain. The money that Americans had to send was called **tax** money. This tax money would help Great Britain get back the money it had spent on the war.

In 1765 the British made a new tax law for the colonies. It was called the **Stamp Act**. The Stamp Act said that Americans had to pay a tax on things made from paper, such as newspapers. A special stamp was placed on the newspapers to show that the tax was paid.

Americans did not like the Stamp Act. They said this tax law was unfair. It was unfair because Americans did not help make the tax law. Some Americans decided not to pay the new taxes. Some Americans burned stamps to show they were angry about the new law.

Americans wanted the same freedom to make laws that the British had. In Great Britain the British helped make their own laws. They did this by voting for leaders who would make laws for them. The British leaders who worked together to make laws for Great Britain were called **Parliament**. Americans wanted to send their own leaders to Great Britain. They wanted these leaders to be in Parliament and make laws. The British would not let Americans make laws in Parliament.

King George III

Parliament Building

Americans burned stamps to show they did not like the Stamp Act.

Parliament wrote more tax laws for the 13 colonies. The British leaders did not let Americans help write any of these laws. Americans did not like the new laws that the British wrote for them.

In 1773 the British made another law. This law said that Americans must pay a tea tax. This meant that Americans had to pay a tax when they paid for their tea. Americans had to send the tax money to Great Britain. Americans were very angry because they did not help write the tea tax law.

Boston was a large **port** city in Massachusetts near the Atlantic Ocean. Three ships with boxes of tea came to Boston. The Americans did not want to pay a tea tax. They did not want the tea. They wanted to send the tea ships back to Great Britain. The British said that Americans had to pay for the tea.

Some Americans decided to throw the boxes of tea into the ocean. One night in 1773, they put on American Indian clothes. They went on the tea ships. The Americans threw every box of tea into the Atlantic Ocean. This is known as the **Boston Tea Party**. The Boston Tea Party made King George very angry.

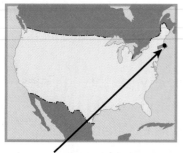

Boston, Massachusetts

At the Boston Tea Party, Americans threw British tea into the ocean.

The first battle of the American Revolution was in Massachusetts.

King George punished the people of Boston. He closed Boston's port. Ships could not come to or go from the port. King George said the port would be closed until Americans paid for all the tea. The king sent many British soldiers to Massachusetts.

The British had made another law that Americans did not like. This law said that Americans must give British soldiers food and a place to sleep. The soldiers paid Americans when they ate and slept in their homes. But Americans did not like the British soldiers. They did not want the soldiers in their homes. King George sent more soldiers to Massachusetts. Americans became angrier and angrier.

The angry Americans formed an army. In 1775 America began to fight Great Britain for freedom. The fighting began in Massachusetts. The British won the first battles. But the Americans would not stop fighting. They were fighting for the same freedom that people had in Great Britain. They wanted the freedom to write their own laws. A war had started in 1775 between Great Britain and America. Americans called this war the **American Revolution**.

⭐ **Read and Remember**

Match Up   Finish each sentence in Group A with words from Group B. Write the letter of the correct answer on the blank line. The first one is done for you.

Group A

1. Great Britain wanted the colonies to help pay for the __C__

2. The new tax laws were not fair to Americans because _____

3. During the Boston Tea Party, Americans went on three British ships and _____

4. After the Boston Tea Party, King George punished Americans by _____

5. In 1775 America began fighting a war with Great Britain that the Americans _____

Group B

a. closing the port of Boston.

b. called the American Revolution.

c. French and Indian War.

d. threw all the tea into the ocean.

e. Americans did not help write the laws in Parliament.

Think and Apply ⭐

Understanding Different Points of View   People can look in different ways at something that happens. Look at these two points of view.

Americans should give British soldiers food.
British soldiers should get their own food.

In 1775 the Americans and the British had different points of view about how to rule the 13 colonies. Read the sentences below. Write **American** next to the sentences that show the American point of view. Write **British** next to the sentences that show the British point of view. The first sentence is done for you.

___British___   1. Only people in Great Britain should write laws in Parliament.

_____   2. Americans should help write their own laws in Parliament.

_____ 3. Americans should not pay a tea tax if they did not help write the tax law.

_____ 4. Americans should pay for all the tea they threw in the ocean.

_____ 5. Americans have enough freedom.

_____ 6. Americans should fight the British for more freedom.

 **Skill Builder**

Reading a Time Line   A **time line** is a drawing that shows years on a line. Look at this time line. Read the time line from left to right.

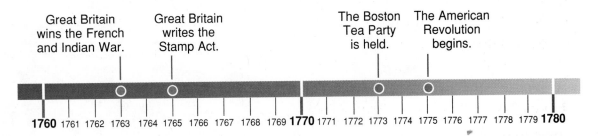

| Great Britain wins the French and Indian War. | Great Britain writes the Stamp Act. | | The Boston Tea Party is held. | The American Revolution begins. |

1760 1761 1762 1763 1764 1765 1766 1767 1768 1769 **1770** 1771 1772 1773 1774 1775 1776 1777 1778 1779 **1780**

The year 1765 comes before 1766, and 1767 comes after 1766.

1. What year comes before 1775? _____

2. What year comes after 1775? _____

Events are sometimes placed on time lines. Read the events on the time line. Then answer each question.

3. When did Great Britain win the French and Indian War? _____

4. When did Great Britain write the Stamp Act? _____

5. When was the Boston Tea Party? _____

Journal Writing

What would you do if you were an American living in the 13 colonies in 1775? Would you help the Americans or the British? Write a paragraph in your journal that tells what you would do and why.

CHAPTER 8

A NEW COUNTRY IS BORN

Think About As You Read

1. Why did Americans write the Declaration of Independence?
2. Why was George Washington a great army leader?
3. How did different people help win the American Revolution?

NEW WORDS

independent
Declaration of Independence
equal
Loyalists
general

PEOPLE & PLACES

Thomas Jefferson
Philadelphia
Friedrich von Steuben
Germany
Thaddeus Kosciusko
Poland
Bernardo de Gálvez
African Americans
James Armistead
Deborah Sampson
Molly Pitcher
Haym Salomon
Jewish American

In 1776 Thomas Jefferson and other leaders wrote the Declaration of Independence.

The American Revolution began in the year 1775. At first Americans were fighting the British because they wanted more freedom. American leaders wrote to King George. They asked him to let Americans write their own laws in Parliament. But King George would not give Americans more freedom. So in 1776 many Americans decided that they wanted the colonies to become **independent**. Independent means "free."

Americans decided to tell the world that the colonies no longer belonged to Great Britain. In 1776 Thomas Jefferson and four other leaders were asked to write the **Declaration of Independence**. The Declaration of Independence was an important paper. It said, "All men are created **equal**."

This means that all people are just as important as a king. The Declaration said all people should have freedom. It also said that the 13 colonies were an independent nation.

The leaders of the 13 colonies met in Philadelphia in the Pennsylvania colony. On July 4, 1776, the leaders agreed to the ideas of the Declaration of Independence.

Some Americans in the colonies did not want the colonies to be free. These people were called **Loyalists**. They fought for Great Britain during the American Revolution.

The American Revolution lasted six years. During that time George Washington was the leader of the American army. The soldiers called him **General** Washington. George Washington was a great leader. He tried to be fair to the soldiers, and he was a good fighter. The Americans lost many battles, or fights. They were often hungry and cold during the winters. But General Washington did not give up. The Americans continued to fight for independence.

Many people tried to help the Americans win the war. France and Great Britain were enemies. French soldiers came to America and fought against the British.

Thomas Jefferson

The Declaration of Independence in 1776

General Washington was the leader of the American army. He is shown here with his soldiers during the cold winter.

James Armistead

Deborah Sampson

People from other nations also helped Americans fight. Friedrich von Steuben came from Germany to help. He taught Americans how to be better soldiers. Thaddeus Kosciusko came from Poland to help Americans fight. Bernardo de Gálvez was the Spanish governor of Louisiana. He led his soldiers against the British.

All kinds of Americans fought together in the war. Farmers, sailors, business owners, and teachers all became soldiers.

About five thousand African Americans fought against the British. They fought in every important battle. James Armistead was a brave African American soldier. He was a spy for the Americans.

Women also helped win the war. They did the farm work when the men were fighting. They grew food for the soldiers. They made clothes for the army. Women also cared for soldiers who were hurt during the war. Deborah Sampson and a few other women dressed like soldiers and fought in the war.

One woman, Molly Pitcher, brought water to American soldiers when they were fighting. Molly's husband, John, was a soldier. One day John was hurt during a battle. He could not fight. Molly took John's place in the battle against the British soldiers.

Molly Pitcher fought in the American Revolution.

Americans cheered for Washington and his soldiers when they won the American Revolution.

Haym Salomon

Haym Salomon was a Jewish American who helped the Americans win. He had left Poland to come to America for freedom of religion. Haym Salomon worked hard and became rich. He knew the American army had little money. The soldiers did not have enough food, clothes, or guns. Some soldiers did not even have shoes. Haym Salomon gave most of his money to the American army. The soldiers bought food, guns, shoes, and clothes with this money.

The American Revolution ended in 1781. The Americans had won. Great Britain and the colonies signed a peace treaty in 1783. People in other countries learned how the Americans won their fight for freedom. Soon people in other countries wanted more freedom, too.

After the war was over, the 13 colonies were independent. The 13 colonies became 13 states. The Americans called their new country the United States of America.

During the war, American leaders had written laws for the United States. But there were problems with those laws. In 1787 American leaders decided to write new laws for their country. In Chapter 11 you will learn how those new laws helped the nation grow.

~ *Diary of a Valley Forge Surgeon* ~

Winters were very hard during the American Revolution. In the winter of 1777, George Washington and his army were at Valley Forge, Pennsylvania. The weather was snowy and very cold. There was very little food. Many of the soldiers did not even have shoes. Albigence Waldo was a surgeon, or a kind of doctor, at Valley Forge. He wrote about that hard winter. Here is part of his diary.

December 12

. . . *We were order'd to march over the River— It snows—I'm Sick—eat nothing. . . . Cold and uncomfortable.*

December 14

. . . *The Army . . . now begins to grow sickly. . . . Yet they still show a spirit . . . not to be expected from so young Troops. I am Sick. . . . Poor food . . . Cold Weather. . . . There comes a bowl of beef soup—full of burnt leaves and dirt. . . . There comes a Soldier, his bare feet are seen thro' his worn out Shoes . . . his Shirt hanging in Strings. . . . I am Sick, my feet lame, my legs are sore. . . .*

December 18

I have pretty well recovered. How much better should I feel, were I assured my family were in health.

troops
soldiers

lame
hurt

recovered
got better

assured
made sure

On a separate sheet of paper, write the answer to each question.

1. What was the army ordered to do on December 12?
2. What was wrong with the soup the soldiers had on December 14?
3. Waldo wrote about a soldier on December 14. What was wrong with the soldier's clothes?
4. On what day did Waldo write that he felt better?
5. Think about Waldo's diary. Why was winter at Valley Forge so hard for the soldiers?

USING WHAT YOU'VE LEARNED

Read and Remember

Finish the Sentence   Draw a circle around the date, word, or words that finish each sentence.

1. Americans in the 13 colonies told the world they were independent in _____ .
   1765   1776   1783

2. Americans agreed to the Declaration of Independence in _____ .
   Boston   Philadelphia   Jamestown

3. _____ taught Americans how to be better soldiers.
   King George   Friedrich von Steuben   Molly Pitcher

4. _____ was a brave African American soldier.
   Haym Salomon   James Armistead   Thomas Jefferson

5. The American Revolution ended in _____ .
   1765   1776   1781

True or False   Write **T** next to each sentence that is true. Write **F** next to each sentence that is false.

_____ 1. Thomas Jefferson helped write the Declaration of Independence.

_____ 2. Some Americans who fought for Great Britain during the American Revolution were called Loyalists.

_____ 3. France sent French soldiers to help the British fight.

_____ 4. Bernardo de Gálvez fought against the British.

_____ 5. Americans called their new country the United Colonies of America.

 Journal Writing

Imagine that you worked for a newspaper in 1776. In your journal, write a short news story about the Declaration of Independence. Tell why Americans wrote the Declaration, and write some of the things it said.

Think and Apply

Drawing Conclusions   Read the first two sentences below. Then read the third sentence. It has an idea that follows from the first two sentences. It is called a **conclusion**.

American farmers and business owners helped win the war.
Women and African Americans helped win the war.

CONCLUSION   Many different Americans were important in the war.

Read each pair of sentences. Then look in the box for the conclusion you can make. Write the letter of the conclusion on the blank. The first one is done for you.

_____d_____ **1.** American colonists wanted more freedom.
King George would not give Americans more freedom.

_____ **2.** Americans called Loyalists fought for Great Britain during the
American Revolution.
The Loyalists liked King George.

_____ **3.** George Washington was fair to the soldiers.
George Washington lost many battles but never gave up.

_____ **4.** Many women grew food and made clothes for the army.
Women took care of soldiers who were hurt.

_____ **5.** Haym Salomon was a rich man.
He knew the American army needed a lot of money.

Conclusions

a. George Washington was a great army leader.

b. Haym Salomon gave money to the American army.

c. Some Americans did not want the colonies to become independent.

d. Americans decided the colonies should be independent.

e. American women helped in many ways during the war.

BENJAMIN FRANKLIN

Think About As You Read

1. What kinds of work did Benjamin Franklin do in Boston and Philadelphia?
2. How did Benjamin Franklin help the city of Philadelphia?
3. How did Benjamin Franklin help the American colonies become independent?

NEW WORDS

printing shop
printer
published
electric sparks
Constitution

PEOPLE & PLACES

Benjamin Franklin

When Benjamin Franklin was a young man, he worked in his brother's printing shop.

Benjamin Franklin was born in Boston, Massachusetts, in 1706. He had 16 brothers and sisters. In those days, people used candles to light their homes. Ben's father earned money by making soap and candles.

Ben was a smart boy. He loved to read books. Ben went to school until he was ten years old. Then Ben made soap and candles with his father.

Ben had an older brother named James. James owned a **printing shop**. When Ben was 12 years old, he went to work for James. Ben became a **printer**. Ben and James **published** a newspaper together. Ben enjoyed his work, but he did not like working with James. Ben decided to run away from Boston.

Ben ran away. He went to Philadelphia, Pennsylvania. Ben worked in a printing shop in Philadelphia. When Ben was 24 years old, he published his own newspaper. People read Ben's newspaper in all 13 American colonies.

Ben wanted Philadelphia to be a better city. Ben started the city's first hospital. He started a fire department. He started a school in Philadelphia. Ben started Philadelphia's first public library.

Ben knew there was something called electricity. He wanted to learn more about electricity. One night there were rain and lightning outside. Ben tied a key to the end of a kite string. He flew the kite outside. Lightning hit the kite. **Electric sparks** jumped off the key. Then Ben knew that lightning is a kind of electricity. People all over America and Europe read about Ben's work with electricity. Ben became famous.

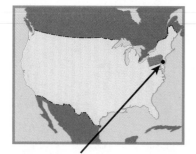

Philadelphia, Pennsylvania

Ben used a kite and a key to show that lightning is a kind of electricity.

Benjamin Franklin

In 1765 Ben and many other Americans became angry about the Stamp Act. Ben traveled to Great Britain. He spoke to Parliament about the Stamp Act. He told the British why the tax law was not fair. Soon after that, the Stamp Act ended.

Ben thought the American colonies should be an independent country. He helped Thomas Jefferson write the Declaration of Independence in 1776. Ben was one of the men who signed the Declaration. Ben wanted to help his country win the American Revolution. He was then seventy years old. Ben went to France. He asked the French people to help the Americans fight. France sent soldiers and ships to the American colonies. France helped the Americans win the war.

In 1787 Ben was 81 years old. He helped write new laws for his country. The new laws were called the **Constitution**. Ben and the other leaders spent four months writing the Constitution in Philadelphia.

Benjamin Franklin died in Philadelphia when he was 84 years old. He was a very famous American. He helped Philadelphia become a great city. He helped the United States become a free country.

Ben went to France to get help for the American soldiers.

USING WHAT YOU'VE LEARNED

⭐ Read and Remember

Find the Answers   Put a check (✓) next to each sentence below that tells how Benjamin Franklin helped Philadelphia and America. You should check four sentences.

_____ **1.** Ben was born in Boston in 1706.

_____ **2.** When Ben was 12, he worked in his brother's printing shop.

_____ **3.** Ben started a hospital and a public library in Philadelphia.

_____ **4.** Ben started a fire department in Philadelphia.

_____ **5.** Ben helped Thomas Jefferson write the Declaration of Independence.

_____ **6.** Ben was about seventy years old during the American Revolution.

_____ **7.** Ben helped write the Constitution in 1787.

_____ **8.** Ben died in Philadelphia when he was 84 years old.

Think and Apply ⭐

Cause and Effect   Match each cause on the left with an effect on the right. Write the letter of the effect on the correct blank.

Cause

1. James and Ben did not get along well, so _____

2. Ben learned how to be a printer in Boston, so _____

3. Lightning hit Ben's kite and sparks flew off the key, so _____

4. Ben wanted the American colonies to become independent, so _____

5. Ben knew that America needed help during the American Revolution, so _____

Effect

a. he signed the Declaration of Independence.

b. he went to France to ask for help.

c. Ben learned that lightning is a kind of electricity.

d. Ben ran away to Philadelphia.

e. he found a job as a printer in Philadelphia.

Skill Builder

Reading a Bar Graph **Graphs** are drawings that help you compare facts. The graph on this page is a **bar graph**. It uses bars of different lengths to show facts. The bar graph below shows the **population** of America's three largest cities in 1776. The number of people in a city is its population.

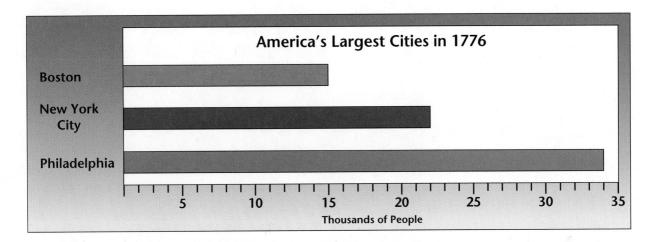

Use the bar graph to answer each question. Draw a circle around the correct answer.

1. How many people lived in Boston in 1776?
   15,000   22,000   34,000

2. How many people lived in Philadelphia in 1776?
   15,000   22,000   34,000

3. What was the population of New York City in 1776?
   5,000   10,000   22,000

4. Which city had the largest population in 1776?
   Boston   New York City   Philadelphia

5. Which of these three cities had the smallest population in 1776?
   Boston   New York City   Philadelphia

Journal Writing

In your journal, write a paragraph telling why Benjamin Franklin was so important in American history.

GEORGE WASHINGTON

Think About As You Read

1. How did George Washington help win the American Revolution?
2. How did George Washington help the United States after the American Revolution?
3. How did Martha Washington help her country?

NEW WORDS

manage
commander in chief
surrendered
Constitutional Convention
First Lady
boundaries

PEOPLE & PLACES

Martha Washington
Mount Vernon
New York City
Trenton, New Jersey
Yorktown
Pierre L'Enfant
Benjamin Banneker
Washington, D.C.

Many Americans call George Washington the "Father of our Country."

George Washington was born in the Virginia colony on February 22, 1732. George's parents owned a large house with a lot of farmland. George was a quiet, shy boy. His father died when George was 11 years old. George then helped his mother **manage** the family farm. He learned how to be a good farmer.

George was a soldier in Virginia. He was tall and strong. In 1754 Great Britain and France began fighting the French and Indian War. George became a leader of the Virginia army. He was 22 years old. George and the Americans helped the British win the war.

In 1759 George married a wealthy woman named Martha. George and Martha Washington lived in a large, beautiful house in Virginia. They called their home Mount Vernon. There were large farms at Mount Vernon. George loved to manage his farms.

In 1775 the American Revolution began. George wanted the American colonies to become independent. He became the **commander in chief** of the American army. This means that he was the leader of all the American soldiers. The soldiers called him General Washington.

George lost a battle in New York City, New York. But he did not give up. He took his army south to Pennsylvania. On Christmas 1776 George took his army to Trenton, New Jersey. Find Trenton on the map on page 60. George knew that the British army there would be having Christmas parties. They would not be ready to fight. George's army surprised the British army. The British army **surrendered**. General Washington won the Battle of Trenton, but the war was not over.

The British and the Americans continued to fight. The American army did not have enough food, clothes, or guns. Many soldiers became sick during the cold winters. Most soldiers liked George Washington. They stayed with him and helped him fight for American freedom.

Martha Washington

Mount Vernon was George and Martha's home in Virginia.

Martha Washington helped the American army during the war. Martha stayed with George during the six cold winters of the American Revolution. She sewed clothes for the soldiers. She fixed their torn shirts and pants. Martha took care of soldiers who became sick or hurt.

In 1781 the Americans won an important battle at Yorktown, Virginia. There the British army surrendered to George Washington. The American Revolution was over. In 1783 Great Britain and the colonies signed a peace treaty. Then General Washington said goodbye to the army. He was ready to go home to Mount Vernon.

Soon the American people needed George Washington again. They wanted him to help write the Constitution. In 1787 American leaders met in Philadelphia to write new laws for the United States. These meetings were called the **Constitutional Convention**. George became president of the Constitutional Convention. He helped the leaders work together to write laws. After that he wanted to return to Mount Vernon. But Americans voted for George to be the new country's first President.

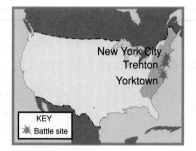

Important battles of the American Revolution

In 1781 British soldiers surrendered to General Washington in Yorktown, Virginia.

In 1789 George Washington became the first President of the United States.

Benjamin Banneker

George Washington became our President in 1789. Martha Washington became the **First Lady**. The government of the United States was in New York City. So George and Martha left Mount Vernon. They traveled to New York City. George was America's hero. As he traveled, crowds everywhere cheered for him.

George wanted the United States to have a new capital city. George found a beautiful place for the capital between Maryland and Virginia. George asked a Frenchman named Pierre L'Enfant to plan the new city.

Benjamin Banneker, a free African American, helped L'Enfant plan the new city. Banneker knew a lot about math and science. He used math and science to help plan the **boundaries** of the new capital. Banneker also wrote to American leaders about ending slavery in the new country. In 1800 the government moved to the new capital. The capital is now called Washington, D.C.

George Washington was President for eight years. As President, George helped the United States become a stronger nation. In 1797 George returned to Mount Vernon. He died at his home in 1799.

George Washington was one of our greatest American leaders. He led our country in war and in peace. Many people call him the "Father of our Country."

Location: Washington, D.C.

The theme of **location** tells where a place is found. Sometimes people use directions to tell where a place is. People also can say what the place is near or what is around it.

Read the paragraphs about Washington, D.C. Study the photo and the map.

After the American Revolution, American leaders decided the United States needed a capital city. The leaders of the United States government would work in the new capital.

In 1790 the leaders decided the capital would be in a southern area of the United States. They wanted the new city to be on the Potomac River. This river flows between Maryland and Virginia. Ships could sail from the Atlantic Ocean into Chesapeake Bay. From the bay, ships could sail on the Potomac River to the new capital. President George Washington picked the area on the Potomac River for the capital city.

Washington, D.C., is not part of any state. It is on land between Maryland and Virginia. The land belongs to the United States government. After George Washington died, the capital was named Washington, D.C. It has been the capital of the United States since 1800.

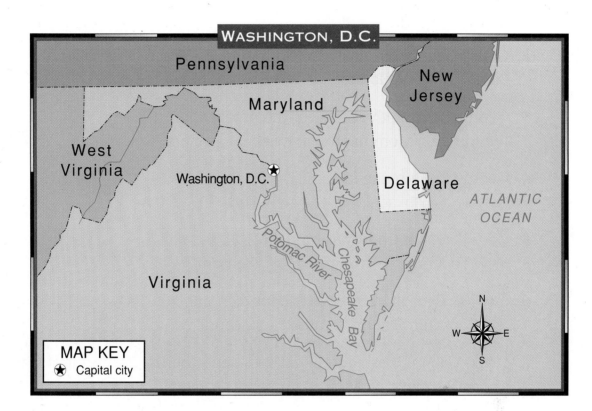

On a separate sheet of paper, write the answer to each question.

1. Look at the map. Between what two states is Washington, D.C., the nation's capital?
2. Along what river is Washington, D.C.?
3. What state is just to the north of Washington, D.C.?
4. What bay leads to the Potomac River?
5. Do you travel north or south to get from Pennsylvania to Washington, D.C.?
6. What are three ways to describe where Washington, D.C., is located?

USING WHAT YOU'VE LEARNED

⭐ Read and Remember

Finish the Sentence   Draw a circle around the word or words that finish each sentence.

1. After his father died, George Washington helped his mother _____ the family farm.
   sell   manage   buy

2. George led the Virginia army in the _____ War.
   British   13 Colonies'   French and Indian

3. George became the _____ of the American army.
   President   commander in chief   captain

4. George lost a battle in _____ .
   Boston   Philadelphia   New York City

5. George won a Christmas battle in _____ .
   New York City   Yorktown   Trenton

6. In 1787 George became president of _____ .
   the Constitutional Convention   Mount Vernon   Georgia

7. When George Washington was President, Martha Washington was _____ .
   general   First Lady   commander in chief

8. Pierre L'Enfant and _____ planned the capital city of Washington, D.C.
   Ben Franklin   James Armistead   Benjamin Banneker

Think and Apply

Sequencing Events   Write the numbers **1, 2, 3, 4,** and **5** next to these sentences to show the correct order.

_____ George Washington became the first President of the United States.

_____ George helped the British win the French and Indian War.

_____ The British army surrendered to George Washington in Yorktown.

_____ George helped write the Constitution.

_____ General Washington led the American army during the revolution.

THE CONSTITUTION

Think About As You Read

1. Why did the United States need a good constitution after the American Revolution?
2. How do Americans write their own laws?
3. How does the Bill of Rights protect your freedom?

NEW WORDS

Congress
Senate
House of Representatives
senators
representatives
Supreme Court
justices
branches of government
freedom of the press
amendments
Bill of Rights

PEOPLE & PLACES

Capitol
White House

Many leaders helped write the United States Constitution.

The American Revolution was won in 1781. The United States was an independent country with 13 states. American leaders had written laws for the country. But there were problems with these first laws. The leaders decided to write a new constitution. In 1787 leaders from 12 of the states went to Philadelphia. There they wrote the United States Constitution at the Constitutional Convention.

Before the American Revolution, Great Britain made laws for the 13 colonies. Americans liked the way the British voted for leaders to write laws in Parliament. The United States leaders planned the Constitution so that Americans could help write their own laws. How do Americans do this?

The United States Constitution in 1787

The Constitution says that Americans should choose, or vote for, people to work for them in their government. Our country's laws are made by men and women in **Congress**. In some ways our Congress is like Great Britain's Parliament. Americans vote for people who will make laws for them in Congress. There are two houses, or parts, of Congress. The **Senate** and the **House of Representatives** are the two houses of Congress.

Men and women who write laws are called **senators** and **representatives**. Every state sends two senators to work in the Senate. States with many people send many representatives to work in the House of Representatives. States with fewer people send fewer representatives to work in the House of Representatives. The senators and representatives meet in a building called the Capitol. The Constitution says that Americans should vote for people to be their senators and representatives. Americans help write their own laws by voting for their senators and representatives.

Congress writes laws in the Capitol building in Washington, D.C. The two houses of Congress are the Senate and the House of Representatives.

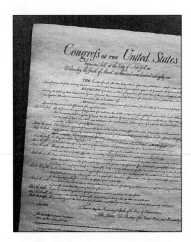

Bill of Rights in 1791

The White House

The Constitution says the President should carry out the country's laws. Americans vote for a President every four years. The President also helps make our laws. The White House is where the President lives and works.

The Constitution also gives the United States its **Supreme Court**. Nine **justices,** or judges, work in the Supreme Court. The Supreme Court justices decide whether our laws agree with the Constitution.

The White House, the Capitol, and the Supreme Court buildings are in the city of Washington, D.C. Important government leaders live and work in the capital city.

Together Congress, the President, and the Supreme Court make up the three **branches of government**. The Constitution gives our country these three branches. Each branch has separate powers. Congress is the branch with the power to write laws. The President leads the branch that has the power to carry out the laws. The Supreme Court is the branch that decides whether the laws agree with the Constitution.

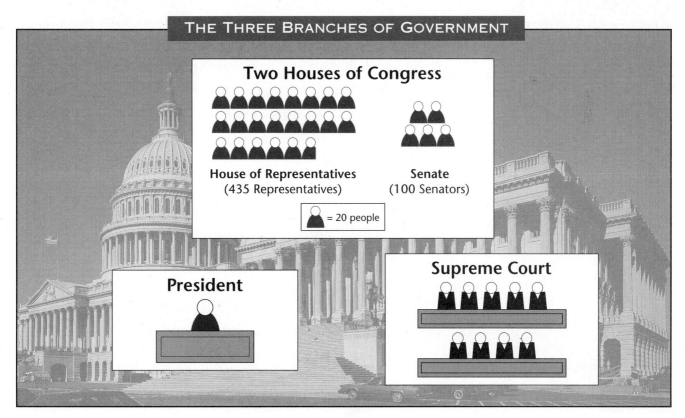

THE THREE BRANCHES OF GOVERNMENT

Two Houses of Congress

House of Representatives
(435 Representatives)

Senate
(100 Senators)

= 20 people

President

Supreme Court

Congress, the President, and the Supreme Court work together in the government.

The President sometimes meets with all the senators and representatives of Congress in the Capitol building.

An American voting

Some of our leaders were not happy with the Constitution when it was written in 1787. The Constitution did not say that Americans had freedom of religion. The Constitution did not say that Americans had **freedom of the press**. "Freedom of the press" means the government cannot tell people what they can say in newspapers and books.

In 1791 our leaders added ten **amendments**, or new laws, to the Constitution. These ten amendments are called the **Bill of Rights**. What are some of these rights? Every American has freedom of religion. Every American has freedom of the press. The Bill of Rights gives every American many freedoms.

Since 1791, seventeen more amendments have been added to the Constitution. Our Constitution now has 27 amendments. These amendments were added because our leaders wanted laws to be fair to all Americans. As our country changes, more amendments may be added to the Constitution.

Today our Constitution is more than 200 years old. The leaders of 1787 gave us good laws. These laws helped the United States become a great country.

Read and Remember

Write the Answer   Write one or more sentences to answer each question.

1. Where did American leaders write the Constitution? _____

_____

2. What do senators and representatives do in Congress? _____

_____

3. How many senators does each state have in the United States Senate? _____

_____

4. What does the President do? _____

_____

5. In what city are the White House, Capitol, and Supreme Court buildings?

_____

6. Why did the leaders add the Bill of Rights to the Constitution? _____

_____

7. What are some of the rights that the Bill of Rights added to the Constitution?

_____

_____

⭐ Think and Apply

Finding the Main Idea   Read each group of sentences below. One of the
sentences is a main idea. Two sentences support the main idea. Write an **M**
next to the sentence that is the main idea in each group.

1. _____   Before the revolution, Great Britain made laws for the colonies.

   _____   Americans made a constitution that said they could help write their
   own laws.

   _____   Americans wanted to help write their own laws.

2. _____ The Constitution says Americans can choose people to work in their government.

_____ Americans vote for their senators and representatives.

_____ Americans vote for their President every four years.

3. _____ The Constitution did not say that Americans had freedom of the press.

_____ In 1791 America's leaders added the Bill of Rights to the Constitution to give Americans many freedoms.

_____ The Constitution did not say that Americans had freedom of religion.

4. _____ The President and the Supreme Court are two branches of the government.

_____ The Senate and the House of Representatives make up one branch of the government.

_____ The United States government has three branches.

5. _____ Americans wrote the Constitution in 1787.

_____ The Constitution has helped our country for more than 200 years.

_____ Americans have added 27 amendments to the Constitution.

Skill Builder

Reading a Diagram   A **diagram** is a picture that helps you understand information. The diagram on page 67 helps you understand our government. Look back at the diagram. Then finish each sentence with a word in blue print.

President   senators   nine   three   435

1. The United States government has _____ branches.

2. The government has one _____ .

3. The government has _____ Supreme Court justices.

4. There are fewer _____ than representatives.

5. There are _____ members of the House of Representatives.

The historical map on this page shows the United States in 1800. Study the map. Then use the words in blue print to finish the story.

Yorktown   **Philadelphia**   **Boston**
New York City   **Washington, D.C.**   **Trenton**

Americans were angry when the British said they had to pay a tax on tea. So Americans in _____ threw tea into the Atlantic Ocean. In 1776 Americans signed the Declaration of Independence in _____ .

During the American Revolution, George Washington won a Christmas battle at _____ . In 1781 the British army surrendered to Washington at _____ . In 1789 Washington went to _____ to become the first President. As President he planned the country's new capital. The name of the capital is _____ . American leaders live and work in the capital city.

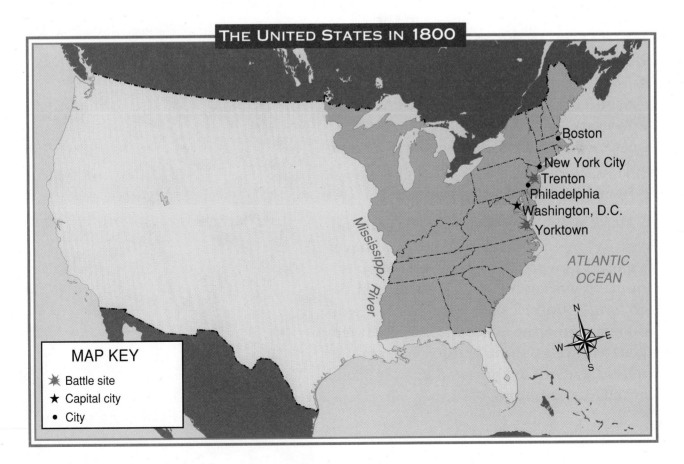

THE UNITED STATES IN 1800

Boston
New York City
Trenton
Philadelphia
Washington, D.C.
Yorktown
Mississippi River
ATLANTIC OCEAN

MAP KEY
✳ Battle site
★ Capital city
● City

UNIT ★ 3

THE UNITED STATES GROWS

Imagine you were an explorer in the year 1803. The United States had bought a large piece of land west of the Mississippi River. President Thomas Jefferson had decided to send people to explore it. Your trip would be long and slow. You would cross mountains and rivers. You would meet many American Indians.

There were many changes in the United States in the early 1800s. The country became much larger. From 1812 to 1814, the United States fought a second war against Great Britain. Americans started working in factories. American cities grew larger. Many people worked to make the United States a better place to live.

What would you have done if you had lived in the early 1800s? Would you have explored new lands in the West? Would you have worked to solve problems in the growing country? As you read Unit 3, you will learn how the United States changed. While you read, think about what you would have done if you had lived in the United States before 1850.

1801
Thomas Jefferson becomes the third President.

1804
Lewis and Clark explore Louisiana.

1812
The War of 1812 begins.

1821
Sequoya makes the first American Indian alphabet.

1829
Andrew Jackson becomes President.

1837
Mount Holyoke Female Seminary opens.

1848
Elizabeth Cady Stanton holds a meeting for women's rights.

1800

1810

1820

1830

1840

1850

1803
The United States buys New Orleans and Louisiana.

1814
Great Britain and the United States sign a peace treaty to end the war.

1825
The Erie Canal is completed.

1838
The Cherokee are forced to move west.

73

THE UNITED STATES DOUBLES IN SIZE

Think About As You Read

1. Why was New Orleans important to the United States?
2. How did the United States double in size in 1803?
3. How did Lewis and Clark help Thomas Jefferson?

NEW WORDS

crops
Louisiana Purchase
doubled

PEOPLE & PLACES

West
Napoleon
Meriwether Lewis
William Clark
York
Rocky Mountains
Pacific Ocean
Sacagawea

An American Indian woman named Sacagawea helped Lewis and Clark travel to the Pacific Ocean.

The man who wrote most of the Declaration of Independence became President of the United States in 1801. Americans voted for Thomas Jefferson to be their third President.

The American Revolution was over. The United States owned all the land east of the Mississippi River except Florida. At first, most Americans lived in the 13 states near the Atlantic Ocean. But every year more Americans moved to the West. By 1800 almost one million Americans lived on the land between the 13 states and the Mississippi River. They built homes and farms. They started new states for the United States. In 1803 the United States had 17 states.

Thomas Jefferson

Napoleon

Sometimes Americans moved to land that was being used by American Indians. There were fights between Indian nations and settlers about who would use the land. Many American Indians were forced to leave their land.

New Orleans was an important port city near the Gulf of Mexico and the Mississippi River. Many American farmers lived near the Mississippi River. They sent their farm **crops** in boats down the Mississippi River to New Orleans. American farmers sold their farm crops in New Orleans. Ships from New Orleans carried the crops to port cities on the Atlantic Ocean.

Spain owned Louisiana and the city of New Orleans. You read about Louisiana in Chapter 6. Spain allowed American ships to use the port of New Orleans. In 1800 Spain gave New Orleans and Louisiana back to France. New Orleans was a French city again. President Jefferson was worried. Perhaps France would not allow Americans to use the port.

President Jefferson knew that American farmers needed the port of New Orleans. He wanted the United States to own New Orleans. Thomas Jefferson decided to offer to buy the city.

Napoleon was the ruler of France. France was fighting many wars in Europe. Napoleon needed money for the

The United States bought New Orleans from France as part of the Louisiana Purchase in 1803.

UNDER MY WINGS EVERY THING PROSPERS

French wars. Jefferson asked Napoleon to sell New Orleans to the United States. Napoleon said he would sell New Orleans and all of Louisiana to the United States for 15 million dollars. In 1803 the United States paid 15 million dollars for Louisiana. Look at the map of the **Louisiana Purchase** on this page. The United States now owned New Orleans and much land to the west of the Mississippi River. The United States **doubled** in size in 1803.

President Jefferson wanted to learn about the land, plants, and animals of Louisiana. He wanted to know about the many Indian nations who lived on this land. Jefferson asked Meriwether Lewis to explore Louisiana. Lewis asked William Clark to explore the new land with him. They formed a group with about 35 men.

Lewis and Clark started their trip across Louisiana in 1804. During the trip Lewis and Clark kept journals. They wrote about the people, plants, animals, and mountains.

An African American named York traveled with Lewis and Clark. York was Clark's slave. He was a good hunter. York

Clark's journal

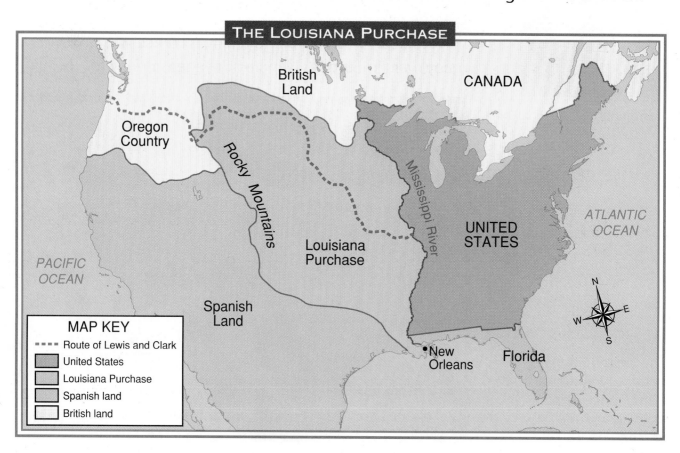

THE LOUISIANA PURCHASE

British Land

CANADA

Oregon Country

Rocky Mountains

Mississippi River

UNITED STATES

ATLANTIC OCEAN

Louisiana Purchase

PACIFIC OCEAN

Spanish Land

New Orleans

Florida

MAP KEY
- - - - Route of Lewis and Clark
United States
Louisiana Purchase
Spanish land
British land

Sacagawea and York helped Lewis and Clark get along with American Indians.

also knew how to get along well with American Indians. He helped Lewis and Clark become friends with more than forty groups of American Indians. Sometime after the trip ended, Clark gave York his freedom.

During their trip Lewis and Clark reached the tall Rocky Mountains. They wanted to cross these mountains and go to the Pacific Ocean. An American Indian woman told Lewis and Clark that she could help them cross the Rocky Mountains. Her name was Sacagawea. She was about 17 years old. Sacagawea said Lewis and Clark needed horses to cross the mountains. She helped them trade with her family for horses.

Sacagawea and her husband led the group across the Rocky Mountains. Sacagawea had a baby boy. She carried the baby on her back. She helped the men find food. The trip across the mountains was slow and dangerous. After many months, the group traveled west to the Pacific Ocean. The map on page 76 shows their route. In 1806 Lewis, Clark, and Sacagawea returned to their homes. They had explored 8,000 miles of land in the West.

Lewis and Clark told Thomas Jefferson about the land they had explored. They made new maps of the West. Thomas Jefferson helped the United States double in size. York, Sacagawea, Lewis, and Clark helped Americans learn about the land in the West.

USING WHAT YOU'VE LEARNED

Read and Remember

True or False   Write **T** next to each sentence that is true. Write **F** next to each sentence that is false.

_____ 1. After the American Revolution, the United States owned all the land east of the Mississippi River.

_____ 2. New Orleans was an important port for American farmers.

_____ 3. Few Americans moved west to the land between the first 13 states and the Mississippi River.

_____ 4. Spain gave Louisiana back to France in 1800.

_____ 5. Napoleon did not want to sell Louisiana to the United States.

_____ 6. The United States paid 15 million dollars for Louisiana and New Orleans.

_____ 7. York and Sacagawea helped Lewis and Clark explore the West.

Skill Builder

Reviewing Map Directions   Study the map on page 76. Choose a word in blue print to finish each sentence. Write the word on the correct blank.

east   south   northwest
west   north   southeast

1. The Pacific Ocean is _____ of the Rocky Mountains.

2. Canada is _____ of the United States.

3. Before the Louisiana Purchase, most Americans lived _____ of the Mississippi River.

4. New Orleans was _____ of the United States.

5. Oregon Country was in the _____ .

6. Florida was _____ of Oregon Country.

Think and Apply

Categories Read the words in each group. Decide how they are alike. Find the best title in blue print for each group. Write the title on the line above each group.

Lewis and Clark   **Napoleon**   **York**
Jefferson   **Sacagawea**

_____

1. wrote most of the Declaration of Independence
   third President of the United States
   wanted the United States to buy Louisiana from France

_____

2. ruler of France
   wanted to sell Louisiana
   needed money for wars in Europe

_____

3. American Indian
   helped Lewis and Clark
   knew how to cross the Rocky Mountains

_____

4. African American slave
   good hunter
   friendly with American Indians

_____

5. explored Louisiana
   kept journals
   made maps of the West

Journal Writing

Look at the list below. If you had gone with Lewis and Clark, which things would you have taken? Choose the five things you think are most important. In your journal, write a paragraph telling why you would have taken each one.

axe   rope   journal   matches   candles
soap   knife   blanket   animal trap   hat

THE WAR OF 1812

Think About As You Read

1. Why did Americans fight a second war against Great Britain?
2. How did Tecumseh try to help American Indians?
3. How did the War of 1812 help the United States?

NEW WORDS

captured
freedom of the seas
navy

PEOPLE & PLACES

James Madison
Tecumseh
Dolley Madison
Fort McHenry
Baltimore
Francis Scott Key
Andrew Jackson

Americans fought the British in the War of 1812 for freedom of the seas.

The United States and Great Britain were fighting again in the year 1812. Why did Americans fight a second war against the British?

Napoleon, the ruler of France, started a war against Great Britain in 1803. The United States wanted to trade with both Great Britain and France. British ships **captured** many American ships that sailed to France. The French did the same thing to ships that sailed to Great Britain. This made Americans very angry. Americans wanted **freedom of the seas**. "Freedom of the seas" means that ships can sail wherever they want.

The British angered Americans in another way. British ships stopped American ships on the ocean. British captains went on the American ships. These captains said that many of the Americans were really British people. They forced these Americans to sail on the British ships. The British made many Americans work for the British **navy**. Americans wanted to trade with France. They did not want their ships captured.

The French agreed to freedom of the seas. The British did not. In 1812 the United States began to fight Great Britain for freedom of the seas. This second war against Great Britain was called the War of 1812. James Madison was President during the War of 1812. He thought the United States would win the war quickly. But the American army and navy were small. The war did not end quickly. Americans fought against the British for more than two years.

During the War of 1812, the United States tried to capture Canada. Canada belonged to Great Britain. The British army in Canada was strong. The United States could not capture Canada.

An American Indian leader named Tecumseh fought for the British during the War of 1812. Tecumseh lived on land between the eastern states and the Mississippi River. He was

James Madison

Tecumseh was killed in a battle during the War of 1812.

Tecumseh

Dolley Madison

angry because each year Americans took more land that belonged to American Indians. The British promised Tecumseh that they would help the American Indians get back their land. So Tecumseh and his people fought for Great Britain. He helped them win some battles in Canada. Tecumseh was killed in a battle during the War of 1812.

The American army had burned some buildings in Canada. The British army decided to burn the American capital city, Washington, D.C. President Madison was not in the city when the British army arrived.

Dolley Madison, the First Lady, was in the White House when Washington, D.C., began to burn. The brave First Lady stayed in the White House. She packed important government papers in a trunk. A famous painting of George Washington was in the White House. Dolley Madison left the burning city with the painting and the government papers. Very soon, British soldiers came to the White House and burned everything still inside. Dolley Madison had saved the painting of Washington and the government papers for the United States.

The British marched into Washington, D.C., and burned many government buildings.

Andrew Jackson and his soldiers won the Battle of New Orleans.

Important battles of the War of 1812

In 1814 the British tried to capture Fort McHenry. This fort guarded the port of Baltimore, Maryland. A large American flag flew over the fort. After the battle, an American named Francis Scott Key saw that this flag still flew over the fort. The flag showed that Americans had won the battle. Francis Scott Key wrote a song about the flag. His song was called "The Star-Spangled Banner." It became our country's song.

The British wanted to capture the port of New Orleans. Andrew Jackson was a general in the American army. He led 5,000 American soldiers in the Battle of New Orleans. These soldiers included people from Europe, American Indians, slaves, and free African Americans. General Jackson won the Battle of New Orleans in January 1815. He did not know that the war had ended already. In December 1814 Great Britain and the United States had signed a peace treaty.

Nothing really changed much because of the War of 1812. Neither country won new land in the war. But Great Britain never again fought against the United States. Great Britain and other countries now knew that the United States was strong enough to fight for what it wanted.

~ Chief Tecumseh's Speech, 1810 ~

There were many American Indians who lived on land between the states and the Mississippi River. In the early 1800s, many American Indian groups were forced to sign treaties with Governor William Henry Harrison. In these treaties, the American Indians gave their land to the United States.

Tecumseh was the chief of the Shawnee, a group of American Indians. He was very angry about the treaties. In 1810 Tecumseh met with Governor Harrison. Tecumseh told Harrison that the United States had no right to take land from American Indians. Here is part of his speech.

Great Spirit
important American Indian god

race
people

miserable
unhappy

unite
join together

> *Once . . . there was no white man on this continent. . . . All belonged to red men, children of the same parents, placed on it by the Great Spirit that made them, to keep it . . . , and to fill it with the same race. Once a happy race—since made miserable by the white people. . . . The way . . . to stop this evil is for all the red men to unite in claiming a common and equal right in the land . . . ; for it . . . belongs to all. . . .*
>
> *The white people have no right to take the land from the Indians, because they had it first; it is theirs. . . . All red men have equal rights to the . . . land. . . . It belongs to the first who sits down on his blanket or skins which he has thrown upon the ground; and till he leaves it, no other has a right.*

On a separate sheet of paper, write the answer to each question.

1. Who was Tecumseh?
2. To whom did Tecumseh give his speech in 1810?
3. What god did Tecumseh believe placed American Indians on the land?
4. Who did Tecumseh say made American Indians unhappy?
5. What did Tecumseh believe American Indians should do to stop Americans from taking their land?
6. Why did Tecumseh believe the land belonged to American Indians?

Read and Remember

Choose the Answer   Draw a circle around the correct answer.

1. What country was Great Britain fighting in 1803?
   the United States   France   Spain

2. What did the United States fight Great Britain for in 1812?
   freedom of the seas   freedom of the press   freedom of religion

3. Who was President during the War of 1812?
   George Washington   Thomas Jefferson   James Madison

4. What did Tecumseh want?
   to be rich   to get back American Indian lands   to go to France

5. Who fought for Great Britain during the War of 1812?
   Tecumseh   Andrew Jackson   James Madison

6. Who saved the painting of George Washington when the British burned Washington, D.C.?
   Dolley Madison   Molly Pitcher   Martha Washington

7. Which country won the battle at Fort McHenry?
   the United States   Great Britain   France

8. Who wrote our country's song, "The Star-Spangled Banner"?
   a British soldier   Francis Scott Key   Dolley Madison

9. Who won the Battle of New Orleans?
   James Armistead   Ben Franklin   Andrew Jackson

Journal Writing

It often took months for mail to get anywhere in the United States. Because of the slow mail, Andrew Jackson didn't know that the War of 1812 had ended. He and his soldiers fought the Battle of New Orleans. Imagine how he felt when he learned that the peace treaty had already been signed. Write four or five sentences in your journal that tell how Jackson must have felt.

Think and Apply

Drawing Conclusions   Read each pair of sentences. Then look in the box for the conclusion you can make. Write the letter of the conclusion on the blank.

1. British ships captured American ships that were sailing to France.
   British captains forced American sailors to work on British ships.

   Conclusion _____

2. Americans wanted Canada to be part of the United States.
   The British army in Canada was too strong.

   Conclusion _____

3. African Americans fought in the United States Army.
   People from Europe fought for the United States.

   Conclusion _____

4. Great Britain and the United States wanted peace.
   Both countries had won and lost many battles.

   Conclusion _____

5. In December 1814 Great Britain and the United States signed a
   peace treaty.
   In January 1815 Andrew Jackson won the Battle of New Orleans.

   Conclusion _____

   a. The United States could not capture Canada.

   b. Great Britain and the United States signed a peace treaty.

   c. Americans wanted freedom of the seas.

   d. Andrew Jackson did not know that the war was over.

   e. Many people helped the United States in the War of 1812.

CHAPTER 14

THE INDUSTRIAL REVOLUTION

Think About As You Read

1. How did the Industrial Revolution begin in the United States?
2. How did canals and railroads help the United States?
3. How did the Industrial Revolution change the United States?

NEW WORDS

Industrial Revolution
goods
invented
cotton gin
mass production
steamboat
steam engine
canals
locomotives

PEOPLE & PLACES

Samuel Slater
Eli Whitney
Francis Cabot Lowell
Robert Fulton
Hudson River
Erie Canal
Lake Erie

After the Industrial Revolution began, people used machines in factories to make goods.

In the 1700s most people wore clothes that were made by hand. They wore shoes that were made by hand, too. Then in 1790 the **Industrial Revolution** began in the United States. It brought many changes to American life.

The Industrial Revolution was a change in the way **goods** were made. Before this revolution, most goods were made by hand at home. After the revolution began, many goods were made by machines in factories.

The Industrial Revolution began in Great Britain. For hundreds of years, the British had made cloth by hand at home. In the 1700s the British **invented** machines to help them make cloth. Soon the British began to use the machines in factories. This was the start of the Industrial Revolution.

Samuel Slater

Eli Whitney

Samuel Slater helped start the Industrial Revolution in the United States. Slater had grown up in Great Britain. He studied how the British built their machines for making cloth. Then he moved to the United States. He built new machines for spinning thread. In 1790 Slater and a partner built a factory where workers could use Slater's spinning machines. Soon the factory was making lots of thread.

Eli Whitney also changed the way goods were made. In 1793 Whitney invented a machine called the **cotton gin**. This machine helped cotton farmers. After cotton was picked, seeds had to be removed from the cotton plant. Before the cotton gin, workers removed the seeds by hand. After all the seeds were removed, cotton could be made into thread. It took a long time to remove the cotton seeds by hand. The new cotton gin removed the seeds quickly. Farmers began to grow much more cotton. The cotton was made into thread in factories.

Eli Whitney helped the Industrial Revolution in another way. He began **mass production**. In mass production, people or machines make many goods that are exactly alike. In 1798 the United States Army needed many new guns. Whitney showed how he could use his machines to make thousands of guns in one factory. All the guns were alike. They had the same parts. If a part for one gun broke, the

Eli Whitney's cotton gin removed seeds from cotton quickly.

gun could be fixed with the same part for another gun. Soon many factories began doing mass production. It became faster and cheaper to make goods.

Francis Cabot Lowell started a factory for making cloth in Massachusetts. Lowell was the first person to put all the machines for making thread and cloth in one factory. He needed workers for his factory. He hired young women to work in his factory. Lowell tried to give his workers good places to live. But the women had to work very hard. They had to work with dangerous machines. They worked in the factory from morning until night. Many other factories hired both women and children.

Many early factories used water power.

Most American factories were built near rivers. Water power from the rivers was used to run the machines. The rivers also were used to move factory goods from one place to another. Ships carried goods on rivers to many parts of the country.

People wanted to travel faster on rivers. In 1807 a man named Robert Fulton sailed a **steamboat** on the Hudson River in New York. A **steam engine** helped the boat move faster. By the 1820s there were many steamboats carrying people and goods on rivers.

In 1807 Robert Fulton sailed his steamboat, the *Clermont*, on the Hudson River.

Soon Americans needed more waterways to move goods. They began to build **canals**. These canals were waterways that joined rivers and lakes. The first big canal was built in New York. It was the Erie Canal. It was finished in 1825. Ships sailed from the Atlantic Ocean into the port of New York City. Then they sailed up the Hudson River. From there ships could sail on the Erie Canal all the way to Lake Erie. The canal was more than 300 miles long. Many new businesses, factories, and cities were built near the Erie Canal. The canal helped New York City become a very large city.

People wanted a better way to travel across land. Wagons were very slow. People began to build railroads. At first, horses pulled the trains. Soon people wanted faster trains. They built trains that were pulled by **locomotives**. Each locomotive had a steam engine. The steam engine made the locomotive move faster than trains pulled by horses.

Locomotive pulling train

The Industrial Revolution helped the growth of American cities. Before 1800, most people were farmers. Most people did not live in cities. In the 1800s more and more people began working in factories. Cities grew around these factories. As time passed, more Americans lived in cities. Fewer people lived on farms. The Industrial Revolution changed life in the United States.

Read and Remember

Find the Answers   Put a check (✓) next to each sentence below that tells about the Industrial Revolution. You should check four sentences.

_____ **1.** In the 1700s the British invented machines that changed how cloth was made.

_____ **2.** Samuel Slater built spinning machines in the United States.

_____ **3.** Cotton seeds are removed from the cotton plant after it is picked.

_____ **4.** Mass production made it faster and cheaper to make goods.

_____ **5.** Before 1800 most people were farmers.

_____ **6.** Wagons are a slow way to travel.

_____ **7.** People built canals and made trains to help move goods quickly.

Think and Apply

Cause and Effect   Match each cause on the left with an effect on the right. Write the letter of the effect on the correct blank.

Cause

1. It took a long time to pick seeds out of cotton, so _____

2. Water power was used to run machines in factories, so _____

3. Francis Cabot Lowell needed workers for his cloth factories, so _____

4. More and more people began working in factories, so _____

Effect

a. he gave jobs to young women.

b. Eli Whitney invented the cotton gin.

c. cities grew around the factories.

d. most factories were built near rivers.

Journal Writing

The Industrial Revolution changed the United States in many ways. Write a paragraph in your journal that tells about two ways the United States changed.

91

Skill Builder

Reading a Line Graph   A **line graph** shows how something changes over time. The line graph below shows how the population of New York City changed from 1790 to 1840. The Erie Canal was finished in 1825. The Industrial Revolution and the Erie Canal helped bring many people to the city. Study the line graph.

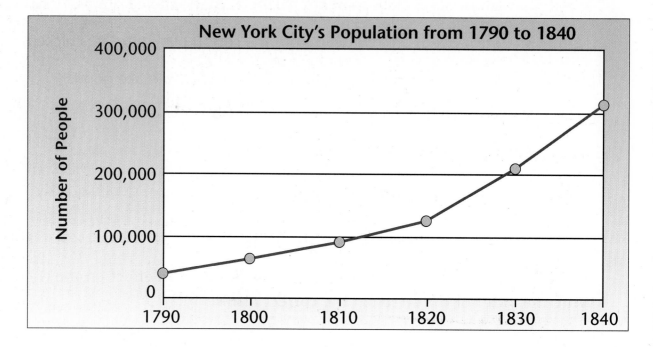

Circle the number or words that finish each sentence.

1. In 1810 New York City's population was about _____ people.
   61,000   96,000   124,000

2. The population was about 203,000 people in _____ .
   1800   1830   1840

3. The line graph shows that many people began to _____ .
   move to the city   move to farms   leave the nation

4. The population _____ between 1790 and 1840.
   stayed the same   grew slowly   grew larger

5. By 1840 the population was about _____ people.
   124,000   313,000   400,000

ANDREW JACKSON

Think About As You Read

1. How did Andrew Jackson become a hero?
2. How did Sequoya help the Cherokee?
3. Why did Osceola fight against the United States Army?

NEW WORDS

border
Trail of Tears
tariffs

PEOPLE & PLACES

North Carolina
South Carolina
Creek
South
Cherokee
Alabama
Sequoya
Indian Territory
Oklahoma
Osceola
Seminole

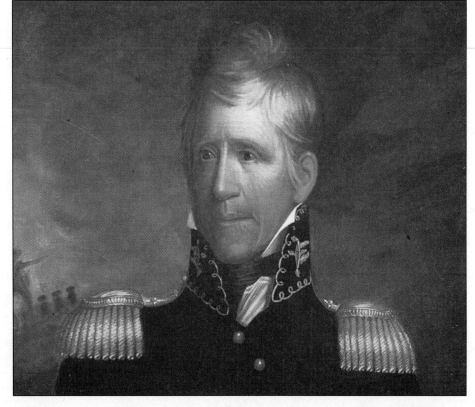

Andrew Jackson became President in 1829. He was called the "People's President."

Andrew Jackson was the seventh President of our country. He was born near the **border** between North Carolina and South Carolina in 1767. Jackson's father died before Jackson was born. In 1780 Jackson fought for America during the American Revolution. He was 13 years old. Jackson's two brothers died during the American Revolution. His mother also died during the war. Jackson had to live by himself when he was only 14 years old. After the war Jackson studied law and became a lawyer.

Andrew Jackson wanted to help his country during the War of 1812. A large group of American Indians called the Creek lived in the South. The Creek helped the British during the War of 1812. Andrew Jackson led his soldiers against the Creek. Americans fought the Creek for many months.

Another group of American Indians was the Cherokee. They helped Americans fight against the Creek. In March 1814 the Creek lost an important battle in Alabama. They surrendered to Andrew Jackson and stopped fighting. The Creek had to give most of their land in Alabama and Georgia to Americans. Jackson and his soldiers also fought American Indians in Florida. Florida belonged to Spain. In 1819 Spain sold Florida to the United States for five million dollars.

Andrew Jackson became a hero. People liked him because he won the battle against the Creek and the Battle of New Orleans. Andrew Jackson became President of the United States in 1829.

Sequoya was a Cherokee who helped Americans fight the Creek. The Cherokee spoke their own language. They did not know how to write their language. The Cherokee, like other American Indians, did not have an alphabet.

Sequoya with his Cherokee alphabet

The United States fought many battles with American Indians.

Sequoya decided to help his people learn to read and write. He carefully studied the Cherokee language. By 1821 Sequoya had made an alphabet for the Cherokee language. His alphabet had 85 letters.

Sequoya helped the Cherokee learn to read and write with his alphabet. The Cherokee started the first American Indian newspaper. They printed books. The Cherokee started schools. Soon almost every Cherokee could read and write Sequoya's alphabet.

Thousands of American Indians lived in the Southeast. Many Americans wanted to own land in the Southeast. President Jackson and these Americans believed that American Indians should move off the land. In 1830 Congress passed a law. It said American Indians must move to land west of the Mississippi River. They had to move to an area called Indian Territory. Today much of this land is part of the state of Oklahoma. President Jackson worked to carry out the new law.

From 1830 to 1839, many thousands of American Indians were forced to move west to Indian Territory. They did not

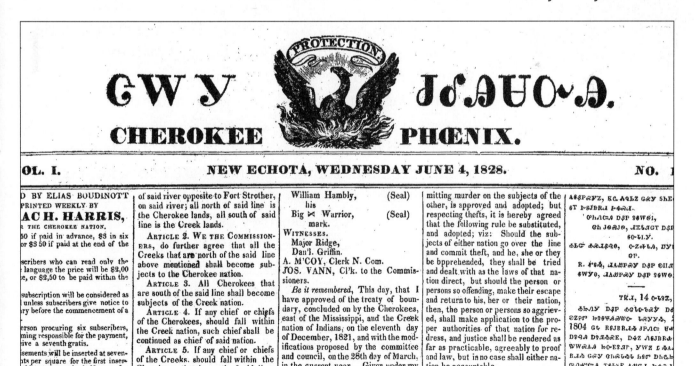

Indian Territory in 1838

The Cherokee started the first American Indian newspaper. It was written in both English and Cherokee languages.

American soldiers captured many Seminole during battles in Florida.

Osceola

want to leave their homes, farms, and villages in the Southeast. The Cherokee called the sad trip to the West the **Trail of Tears**. Many American Indians became sick and died during the long, hard trip.

Osceola was a brave American Indian who would not move west. Osceola was the leader of the Seminole in Florida. He led his people in battles against the American army. After many battles Osceola was captured. He was sent to jail. He became very sick and died. After Osceola died most of the Seminole moved west. Some Seminole stayed in Florida.

While Jackson was President, some states did not want to obey tax laws made by Congress. People in South Carolina did not want to pay **tariffs**. A tariff is a tax on goods from other countries. Tariffs make goods from other countries cost more money. The southern states bought many goods from Europe. They did not want to pay tariffs on the goods. Andrew Jackson said that all states must obey the laws of the United States. He said that he would send United States soldiers to South Carolina. South Carolina obeyed the laws. The tariffs were paid.

Andrew Jackson was President for eight years. He was called the "People's President." He believed that all people, both rich and poor, should work for their country. Jackson died in 1845.

Movement: The Trail of Tears

The theme of **movement** tells how people, goods, and ideas move from one place to another. In the 1800s people traveled on horses, wagons, boats, or trains. Goods were sent on wagons, trains, or ships. Ideas were told by one person to another. Some ideas were shared in newspapers.

Read the paragraphs about the Trail of Tears. Study the photo and the map.

In 1838 most Cherokee lived in Georgia and nearby states. Other American Indians of the Southeast had been forced to move west to Indian Territory before 1838. The Cherokee were the last Indian nation to leave the Southeast.

In May 1838 the United States Army began to force about 17,000 Cherokee to leave their homes. The Cherokee were divided into groups. Some groups used land routes. They traveled through many states to reach Indian Territory. Many people walked to Indian Territory. Some rode on horses. Older people traveled in wagons. Other groups used a water route. They traveled in boats on different rivers to Indian Territory. Both routes were very dangerous.

In June 1838 the first group of Cherokee began the long trip west. The trip was more than 800 miles. The trip was hard. There

was not enough food and water. The winter was very cold. People did not have enough warm clothes and blankets. About 4,000 Cherokee died on the way to Indian Territory. The Cherokee called this hard trip the Trail of Tears. In March 1839 the last group on the Trail of Tears reached Indian Territory.

The Cherokee brought their language, religion, songs, and customs to Indian Territory. They continued to tell old Cherokee stories to their children. They started a Cherokee capital city called Tahlequah. Today more Cherokee live in Oklahoma than in any other state.

THE TRAIL OF TEARS

Indian Territory (Oklahoma)
Missouri
Illinois
Kentucky
Tahlequah
Arkansas
River
Tennessee
River
Arkansas River
Chattanooga
Mississippi
Tennessee
Fort Payne
TEXAS
MAP KEY
— Land route
— Water route
Louisiana
Mississippi
Alabama
Georgia
N W E S

On a separate sheet of paper, write the answer to each question.

1. Some Cherokee rode horses along the land routes. How did other Cherokee travel on land?
2. What did Cherokee travel in if they took a water route?
3. How did children in Indian Territory learn old Cherokee stories?
4. Look at the map. What are five states the Cherokee traveled through on their land routes?
5. What were three rivers the Cherokee used on their water route?

⭐ Read and Remember

Finish the Story   Use the words in the first box to finish the first paragraph. Use the words in the second box to finish the second paragraph. Write the words you choose on the blank lines.

Paragraph 1	Paragraph 2
Creek	newspaper
Spain	west
five	Florida
Florida	Army
Territory	Osceola
Trail of Tears	alphabet
tariff	Cherokee

During the War of 1812, Andrew Jackson fought against a group of American Indians called the _____ . Jackson also fought against American Indians in _____ . In 1819 _____ sold Florida to the United States for _____ million dollars. As President, Jackson said all states must obey the _____ laws. Jackson also forced American Indians to move west to Indian _____ . Many American Indians became sick and died as they moved west. The Cherokee called the sad trip to the West the _____ .

Two famous American Indians lived during the time of Andrew Jackson. Sequoya was a _____ . He helped his people by making the first American Indian _____ . It had 85 letters. The Cherokee used it to print books and a _____ . The famous leader of the Seminole in Florida was _____ . This brave leader would not move _____ . He fought many battles against the United States _____ . After Osceola died, most American Indians in _____ were forced to move west.

Think and Apply

Fact or Opinion   Read each sentence below. Write an **F** next to each sentence that tells a fact. Write an **O** next to each sentence that tells an opinion. You should find six opinions.

_____ 1. Andrew Jackson fought the Creek.

_____ 2. Andrew Jackson was a good President.

_____ 3. The United States paid too much money to Spain for Florida.

_____ 4. Sequoya was a Cherokee.

_____ 5. Sequoya spent too much time making the alphabet.

_____ 6. The Cherokee made the first American Indian newspaper.

_____ 7. The Cherokee newspaper had many interesting stories.

_____ 8. The United States Congress can write tax laws.

_____ 9. States should not have to pay tariffs.

_____ 10. Andrew Jackson was a better President than Thomas Jefferson.

_____ 11. Jackson believed that American Indians should move west of the Mississippi River.

_____ 12. The Cherokee moved to Indian Territory.

_____ 13. Osceola wanted to stay in Florida.

_____ 14. Many American Indians died during the long, hard trip to Indian Territory.

 # Journal Writing

Imagine that you and your family are American Indians. You are forced to move west. Think about how you would feel. In your journal, write four or five sentences telling about your feelings. Be sure to tell why you feel the way you do.

CHAPTER 16

AMERICANS WORK FOR REFORM

Think About As You Read

1. What was education like in the early 1800s?
2. How did some Americans help education?
3. How did other Americans work for reform?

NEW WORDS

reform
education
disabilities
abolitionists
mental illness

PEOPLE & PLACES

Horace Mann
Emma Willard
Mary Lyon
Mount Holyoke Female Seminary
Oberlin College
Ohio
Thomas Gallaudet
Connecticut
William Lloyd Garrison
Frederick Douglass
North
Dorothea Dix
Elizabeth Cady Stanton
Seneca Falls

Frederick Douglass worked to end slavery.

Should there be free schools for all children? Should there be laws to end slavery? Should men and women have the same rights? People asked these questions in the early 1800s. Many people answered "no" to these questions. Other people wanted to improve the country. These Americans began to work for **reform**.

In the early 1800s, there were no laws that said children must go to school. Many children worked on farms and in factories. Children from rich families went to fine private schools. But children from poor families did not attend good schools. They often went to public schools that had only one big classroom. All grades were in the classroom. These schools had only one teacher. There were few books. There were not very many high schools.

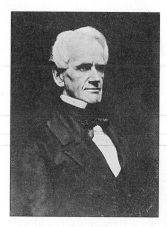

Horace Mann

Mary Lyon

Horace Mann worked to improve public schools in Massachusetts. He worked to have the state pay for children to go to public schools. People built bigger schools that had many classrooms. People built more high schools. Mann started the first school to teach people how to be good teachers. He also helped teachers earn higher pay.

Massachusetts had better schools because of Horace Mann. Other states began to improve their schools, too. States passed laws that said children must go to school.

At that time girls could not get the same **education** that boys could. Often they could only go to school if there was room. This was usually in the summer. Girls were not taught science or math. Girls were not allowed to go to college.

Emma Willard helped girls get a better education. She started the first high school for girls.

Mary Lyon also helped women get a better education. She decided to start a college for women. It was called Mount Holyoke Female Seminary. Mount Holyoke opened in Massachusetts in 1837. Women at Mount Holyoke studied the same subjects that men studied in other colleges.

Soon other colleges for women were started. Women were allowed to study in some colleges with men. Oberlin College in Ohio became the first college for men and women. It also had many African American students.

Mount Holyoke Female Seminary later became Mount Holyoke College.

At first there were few schools for children with **disabilities**. Thomas Gallaudet believed deaf children should go to school. In 1817 he started a free school for deaf children in Connecticut.

In the 1830s, there were more than two million African American slaves. Most of them lived in the South. Some Americans believed slavery was wrong. They wanted all slaves to be free. They wanted new laws to end slavery. The people who worked to end slavery were called **abolitionists**. William Lloyd Garrison became an abolitionist leader. He published a newspaper about ending slavery.

Frederick Douglass was an African American abolitionist. Douglass had been a slave. He escaped to the North and became free. Douglass gave many speeches. Again and again he told people why slavery was wrong. Many people heard Douglass and became abolitionists.

Dorothea Dix was another American who worked for reform. Dix visited many jails. She worked to make jails better for prisoners. Dix also saw that many prisoners were in jails because they had **mental illness**. She said these people should not be in jail. Dix said people with mental illness should be treated in hospitals. She helped start hospitals to care for people with mental illness.

Dorothea Dix

William Lloyd Garrison published this newspaper about ending slavery.

Elizabeth Cady Stanton spoke about women's rights at a meeting in Seneca Falls in 1848.

Elizabeth Cady Stanton

In the 1800s the fight for women's rights began. Some people felt that women were not treated fairly. Women were not allowed to vote. Married women had to give their money to their husbands. Women could not get good jobs. They could not become doctors or lawyers. Women who worked earned much less money than men did.

Some women abolitionists decided that women should have the same rights that men had. They wanted women to have the right to vote. Elizabeth Cady Stanton was an abolitionist. She was also one of the leaders in the fight for women's rights.

In 1848 Stanton helped plan the first large meeting about women's rights. The meeting was in Seneca Falls, New York. About 240 women and men came to the meeting. Stanton gave a speech. She said women should be allowed to vote. She told why women needed more rights. Frederick Douglass and other people joined the fight for women's rights. Slowly, women did win more rights. In Book 2 you will learn how women won the right to vote in 1920.

Many people in the United States worked for reform in the 1800s. They wanted Americans to have better lives.

⭐ Read and Remember

Match Up   Finish each sentence in Group A with words from Group B. Write the letter of the correct answer on the blank line.

Group A

1. In the early 1800s, there were not enough good _____ .

2. Thomas Gallaudet started a free school for _____ .

3. Women could not become doctors or _____ .

4. Elizabeth Cady Stanton said women should be allowed _____ .

Group B

a. to vote

b. deaf children

c. public schools

d. lawyers

Think and Apply ⭐

Finding the Main Idea   Read each group of sentences below. One of the sentences is a main idea. Two sentences support the main idea. Write an **M** next to the sentence that is the main idea in each group.

1. _____   There were problems in American education in the 1800s.

   _____   There were no laws that said children must go to school.

   _____   There were few schools for children with disabilities.

2. _____   Girls were not taught science and math.

   _____   Only boys were allowed to go to college.

   _____   Girls did not get the same education that boys did.

3. _____   Emma Willard started the first high school for girls.

   _____   People tried to help girls get a better education.

   _____   Mary Lyon started Mount Holyoke Female Seminary.

4. _____   William Lloyd Garrison began a newspaper about ending slavery.

   _____   Frederick Douglass spoke about why slavery was wrong.

   _____   Some Americans wanted to end slavery.

Skill Builder

Reading a Chart A **chart** lists a group of facts. Charts help you learn facts quickly. Read the chart below to learn how some Americans worked for reform in the 1800s.

Americans Who Worked for Reform in the 1800s		
Name	**Place**	**Important Work**
Horace Mann	Massachusetts	Mann improved education in public schools in Massachusetts.
Mary Lyon	Massachusetts	Lyon started Mount Holyoke Female Seminary for women.
Thomas Gallaudet	Connecticut	Gallaudet started the first school for deaf children in the United States.
Frederick Douglass	New York and other states	Douglass was an abolitionist. He worked to end slavery.
Dorothea Dix	Massachusetts	Dix helped start hospitals to treat people with mental illness.
Elizabeth Cady Stanton	New York	Stanton worked for women's rights.

Draw a circle around the words that finish each sentence.

1. To read the names of people who worked for reform, read the chart from _____ .
   left to right   top to bottom   the middle .

2. To learn all about Mary Lyon, read the chart from _____ .
   left to right   top to bottom   bottom to top

3. The person who was an abolitionist was _____ .
   Mary Lyon   Dorothea Dix   Frederick Douglass

4. The person who improved public schools in Massachusetts was _____ .
   Thomas Gallaudet   Horace Mann   Dorothea Dix

5. Elizabeth Cady Stanton worked for _____ .
   women's rights   better schools   hospitals for mental illnesses

Study the time line on this page. Then use the words and date in blue print to finish the story. Write the words and date you choose on the correct blank lines.

cities	**Louisiana**	**reform**
1812	**women's rights**	**doubled**
Cherokee	**Industrial Revolution**	**factory**

Many changes took place in the United States as it grew. The United States

_____ its size when it bought _____ from

France in 1803. The United States showed it was strong when it fought a

second war against Great Britain from _____ to 1814. Many

Americans wanted to own American Indian land. American Indians were forced

to move west. The _____ were forced to move to Indian

Territory in 1838.

The _____ began in the United States in 1790 when Samuel

Slater built a _____ for spinning thread. During the 1800s

fewer people lived on farms. More Americans moved to _____.

People built steamboats, canals, and railroads to help move goods. Many people

worked for _____ in the United States. Elizabeth Cady Stanton

gave a speech about _____ in Seneca Falls in 1848.

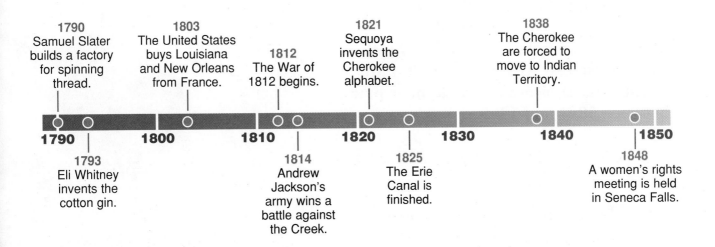

1790
Samuel Slater builds a factory for spinning thread.

1803
The United States buys Louisiana and New Orleans from France.

1812
The War of 1812 begins.

1821
Sequoya invents the Cherokee alphabet.

1838
The Cherokee are forced to move to Indian Territory.

1790 **1800** **1810** **1820** **1830** **1840** **1850**

1793
Eli Whitney invents the cotton gin.

1814
Andrew Jackson's army wins a battle against the Creek.

1825
The Erie Canal is finished.

1848
A women's rights meeting is held in Seneca Falls.

THE NATION
GROWS AND DIVIDES

Imagine living in the United States in 1860. Everyone believes there will be a war between the northern states and the southern states. You must choose a side to fight for in this war. You might have to fight against your own family during the war. You might have to fight against your best friend. Thousands will die during the Civil War.

The years between 1821 and 1865 were years of great change. Many Americans moved west. Areas in the West became new states. The problem of slavery also grew. The northern states did not like slavery. The southern states said they needed slaves. In 1861 the terrible Civil War began.

What would you have done if you had lived between 1821 and 1865? Would you have moved west? Would you have fought for the northern states or for the southern states? As you read Unit 4, think about what choices you would have made between 1821 and 1865.

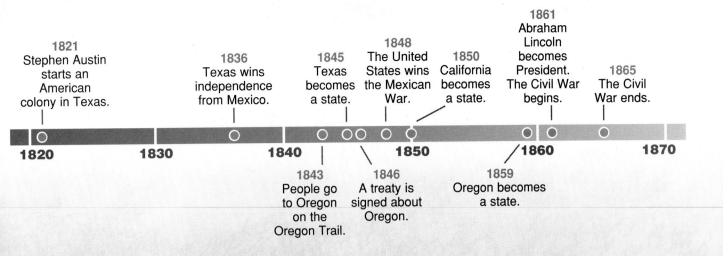

1821
Stephen Austin starts an American colony in Texas.

1836
Texas wins independence from Mexico.

1845
Texas becomes a state.

1848
The United States wins the Mexican War.

1850
California becomes a state.

1861
Abraham Lincoln becomes President. The Civil War begins.

1865
The Civil War ends.

1820   1830   1840   1850   1860   1870

1843
People go to Oregon on the Oregon Trail.

1846
A treaty is signed about Oregon.

1859
Oregon becomes a state.

CHAPTER 17

INDEPENDENCE FOR TEXAS

Think About As You Read

1. Why did Americans want to settle in Texas?
2. What problems did Americans and Mexicans have in Texas?
3. How did Texas become free from Mexico?

NEW WORDS

fort
Texas Revolution
republic

PEOPLE & PLACES

Moses Austin
Stephen Austin
Mexicans
German Americans
Asian Americans
Texans
Santa Anna
Alamo
Suzanna Dickenson
José Antonio Navarro
Lorenzo de Zavala
Sam Houston
San Jacinto River
Republic of Texas

Many Americans and Mexicans moved to Texas in the 1800s.

Mexico belonged to Spain for 300 years. In 1821 Mexico became an independent country. At that time, Texas was part of Mexico.

Moses Austin wanted to start a colony for Americans in Texas. He died before he could start the colony. His son, Stephen Austin, decided to continue his father's plan to settle Texas. Few Mexicans lived in Texas. So the leaders of Mexico wanted Americans to move to Texas.

Stephen Austin started an American colony in Texas in 1821. The settlers liked Texas. The land was good for growing cotton. It was also good for raising cattle. African Americans, German Americans, and Asian Americans moved to Texas. Jewish Americans and many people from Europe also settled in Texas. More people from Mexico went to

Stephen Austin

live in Texas. By 1830 there were many more Americans than Mexicans in Texas. People who live in Texas are called Texans.

Many Mexicans were angry that Americans brought slaves to Texas. Mexican law said no one could own slaves in Texas. Mexicans wanted the Americans to obey this law. But the Americans did not listen.

Mexico's leaders were worried that Texas might want to become part of the United States. In 1830 Mexico made a new law. The law said that Americans could no longer come to live in Texas. Americans in Texas did not like this law.

Texans did not like other Mexican laws. They did not like the law that said Texans must speak Spanish. Another Mexican law said settlers must be Catholic. Texans wanted to help write laws for Texas. Mexico would not let the settlers make laws for Texas.

The Mexican government became angry with the new settlers. The government was angry that slaves were brought to Texas. It was angry that few settlers had become Mexicans. Few Texans spoke Spanish. Many Texans were not Catholic.

Stephen Austin sold land to many families who wanted to move to Texas.

Santa Anna

Suzanna Dickenson

José Antonio Navarro

Santa Anna and his soldiers attacked the Texans at the Alamo.

Mexican soldiers went to Texas to force the Texans to obey Mexican laws. This made the Texans angry. Some Texans began to fight the Mexican soldiers.

Santa Anna was the Mexican president. He led his army against the Texans. In 1836 there were about 180 Texan soldiers in a mission called the Alamo. The Texans used the Alamo as a **fort**. Santa Anna and about 4,000 Mexican soldiers attacked the Alamo. The Texans were very brave. They fought for 13 days. Santa Anna won the Battle of the Alamo. His army killed every Texan soldier.

Some of the Texan soldiers had brought their wives and children to the Alamo. One of these wives was Suzanna Dickenson. After the battle, Santa Anna sent her to tell other Texans not to fight against Mexico.

Texan leaders met in March 1836 while the soldiers were fighting at the Alamo. The leaders wrote a declaration of independence for Texas. This declaration said that Texas was no longer part of Mexico.

Some Mexican Texans also wanted an independent Texas. José Antonio Navarro was a Mexican who was born

Santa Anna surrendered to Sam Houston after the battle at the San Jacinto River.

Lorenzo de Zavala

Texas flag

Republic of Texas

in Texas. He was a friend of Stephen Austin. He signed the Texas Declaration of Independence. He later helped write a new constitution for Texas. Lorenzo de Zavala was born in Mexico. He came to live in Texas with his family. De Zavala also signed the Texas Declaration of Independence. He told all Texans to fight for freedom.

Sam Houston became the commander in chief of the Texas army. He learned about the Battle of the Alamo from Suzanna Dickenson. Sam told his soldiers to remember the brave people who died at the Alamo.

On April 21, 1836, Sam Houston led the Texans against Santa Anna's army. They fought at the San Jacinto River. "Remember the Alamo!" Houston's soldiers shouted as they fought the Mexican soldiers. The battle lasted only 18 minutes. The Texans won. Santa Anna surrendered to Sam Houston. Texas was now free. The Texans called their war against Mexico the **Texas Revolution**.

Texas was no longer part of Mexico, and Texas was not part of the United States. Texas became a **republic**. A republic is an independent country. Sam Houston became the first president of the Republic of Texas. Lorenzo de Zavala became the vice president.

Texans wanted Texas to become part of the United States. But they would have to wait almost ten more years before Texas became a state.

~ Letters from William Barrett Travis ~

William Barrett Travis led the Texan soldiers at the Battle of the Alamo. On March 6, 1836, Santa Anna and his large army captured the Alamo. They killed Travis and the other Texan soldiers. During Travis's last days at the Alamo, he wrote letters asking Americans and Texans to help. Here are parts of three of his letters.

February 23, 1836

We have removed all our men into the Alamo. . . . We hope you will send us all the men you can spare promptly. . . . We have but little provisions. . . .

February 24, 1836

. . . The enemy has demanded a surrender. . . . I shall never surrender. . . . I call on you . . . to come to our aid. . . . Victory or Death. . . .

March 3, 1836

I am still here. . . . I have held this place 10 days against . . . 1,500 to 6,000, and shall continue to hold it till I get relief from my countrymen. . . .

Make a declaration of independence, and we will then understand, and the world will understand, what we are fighting for. . . . Under the flag of independence, we are ready to peril our lives. . . .

promptly
soon

provisions
food

victory
a win

relief
help

peril
put in danger

On a separate sheet of paper, write the answer to each question.

1. Where were Travis and his men on February 23, 1836?
2. On February 23 what did Travis say he hoped Texans would do?
3. What did the enemy want Travis to do on February 24?
4. How many days had Travis been inside the Alamo as of March 3?
5. How many Mexican soldiers did Travis think his army was fighting on March 3?
6. On March 3 what did Travis tell Texans to do?

⭐ Read and Remember

Finish Up Choose the best word or words in blue print to finish each sentence. Write the word or words you choose on the correct blank.

| Sam Houston | Santa Anna | Texas Revolution |
| Alamo | de Zavala | Stephen Austin |

1. _____ started an American colony in Texas.

2. José Antonio Navarro and Lorenzo _____ were Mexican Texans who signed the Texas Declaration of Independence.

3. The leader of the Texas army and the first president of the Republic of Texas was _____ .

4. The leader of the Mexican army was President _____ .

5. The war for Texan independence was called the _____ .

6. About 180 Texan soldiers died at the _____ .

Think and Apply ⭐

Understanding Different Points of View Mexicans and Texans had different points of view about Texas. Read the sentences below. Write **Texan** next to the sentences that show the Texan point of view. Write **Mexican** next to the sentences that show the Mexican point of view.

_____ 1. People in Texas should obey Mexican laws.

_____ 2. People in Texas should write their own laws.

_____ 3. Everyone in Texas must be Catholic.

_____ 4. Americans in Texas do not have to be Catholic.

_____ 5. Americans can bring slaves to Texas.

_____ 6. Americans cannot have slaves in Texas.

_____ 7. Americans should speak Spanish in Texas.

_____ 8. Americans can speak English in Texas.

CHAPTER 18

THE UNITED STATES GROWS LARGER

Think About As You Read

1. What was Manifest Destiny?
2. How did the Mexican War help the United States grow larger?
3. How did Mexican Americans help the United States?

NEW WORDS

Manifest Destiny
citizens
Mexican Cession
Gadsden Purchase
property

PEOPLE & PLACES

James Polk
Rio Grande
Mexico City
Nevada
Utah
Arizona
Mexican Americans

When the flag of the Republic of Texas was lowered, Texas became the twenty-eighth state in the United States.

In Chapter 17 you read that Texans won their war against Mexico and started a republic. Santa Anna had surrendered to the Texans. But Mexican leaders did not accept his surrender. The Mexicans said that Texas was still part of Mexico. Texans wanted Texas to become part of the United States. The Mexicans said there would be a war if Texas became part of the United States.

Many Americans wanted Texas to become a state. They believed in an idea called **Manifest Destiny**. Manifest Destiny meant the United States should rule land from the Atlantic Ocean to the Pacific Ocean. This idea also meant that the United States should become a larger and stronger country.

116

James Polk

Texas land claimed
by Mexico

James Polk became President in 1845. The new President believed in Manifest Destiny. He wanted Texas to become a state. He also tried to buy California and New Mexico from Mexico. But Mexico refused to sell its land.

In 1845 the United States Congress voted for Texas to become a state. This made the Mexican government angry.

In 1846 a war started between the United States and Mexico. The two countries did not agree on the border for Texas. The United States said a river called the Rio Grande was the southern border for Texas. Mexico said Texas should be smaller. The Mexicans said that much of the land north of the Rio Grande belonged to Mexico.

The United States and Mexico sent soldiers to the Rio Grande. The soldiers began to fight. This war was called the Mexican War. During the war American soldiers captured California and New Mexico. The Mexican soldiers were brave. They did not stop fighting. Americans and Mexicans continued to fight. In 1847 American soldiers went into Mexico. They captured Mexico City, the capital of Mexico. Soon the Mexicans surrendered. The war was over.

American soldiers stand in the center of Mexico City after capturing this capital city of Mexico.

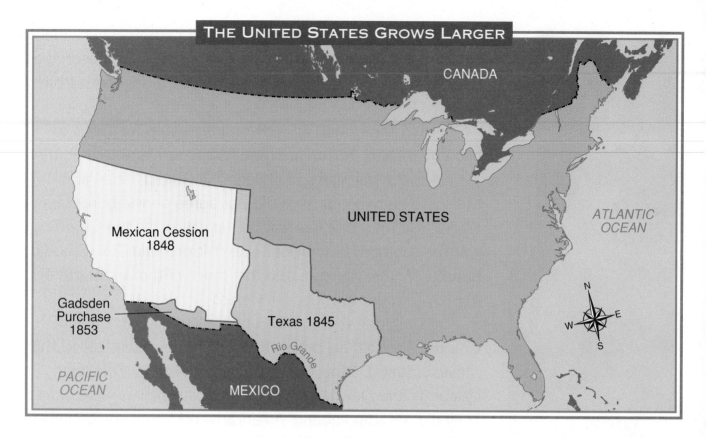

CANADA

UNITED STATES

ATLANTIC OCEAN

Mexican Cession 1848

Gadsden Purchase 1853

Texas 1845

Rio Grande

N
W E
S

PACIFIC OCEAN

MEXICO

The leaders of the United States and Mexico signed a peace treaty in 1848. The treaty gave the United States a large area of Mexican land. It also said that Texas belonged to the United States. The Rio Grande became the border between Texas and Mexico. The treaty also said that Mexicans in the Southwest could become American **citizens**. The United States gave Mexico 15 million dollars for land taken during the war.

The land that the United States got in 1848 was called the **Mexican Cession**. Find the Mexican Cession on the map above. California, Nevada, Utah, Arizona, and New Mexico were five new states made from the Mexican Cession. The United States now owned land from the Atlantic Ocean to the Pacific Ocean.

Americans wanted a railroad across the southern part of the United States. The land south of the Mexican Cession was a good place for a railroad. In 1853 the United States gave Mexico 10 million dollars for the land in the **Gadsden Purchase**. Find the Gadsden Purchase on the map above. Years later, Americans built a railroad across the Gadsden Purchase.

Mexicans in the Southwest became American citizens after the Mexican War. They were called Mexican Americans.

Mexican Americans helped their new country. They taught Americans how to grow food on land where there was little rain. Mexican Americans helped build railroads for the United States. They helped other Americans look for gold and silver in the Southwest. They taught Americans how to be cowboys.

Mexican Americans helped the United States change a law that was unfair to women. Before the Mexican War, a married American woman could not own **property**. Her husband owned everything. Mexican law was fairer to women. Mexican women owned property together with their husbands. After the Mexican War, Americans changed their law so that women could own property with their husbands.

The land of the United States went from the Atlantic Ocean to the Pacific Ocean. The United States had become a strong country with a lot of new land and many new people.

Mexican Americans in the Southwest taught Americans many things, including how to be cowboys.

⭐ Read and Remember

Choose the Answer Draw a circle around the correct answer.

1. Which President believed in Manifest Destiny?
   James Madison   Andrew Jackson   James Polk

2. When did Texas become a state?
   1776   1845   1900

3. What city did American soldiers capture during the Mexican War?
   Boston   Washington, D.C.   Mexico City

4. How much did the United States pay for the Mexican Cession?
   5 million dollars   15 million dollars   30 million dollars

5. Which three states were among the five made from the Mexican Cession?
   California, New Mexico, Arizona   New York, New Jersey, Florida
   Texas, Mississippi, Oklahoma

6. Which river became the border for Texas?
   Mississippi River   St. Lawrence River   Rio Grande

7. What land did the United States buy in 1853?
   Louisiana Purchase   Gadsden Purchase   Florida

8. Why did the United States want the Gadsden Purchase?
   for its water   for a railroad   for a park

Skill Builder

Reviewing Map Directions Look back at the map on page 118. Draw a circle around the word that finishes each sentence.

1. The Gadsden Purchase is _____ of Mexico.
   east   south   north

2. The Pacific Ocean is _____ of the Mexican Cession.
   southeast   east   west

3. The Rio Grande is _____ of the Gadsden Purchase.
   northwest   southwest   east

4. The Mexican Cession is _____ of the Gadsden Purchase.

south   southeast   north

5. Mexico is _____ of the United States.

south   north   west

6. Texas is _____ of the Gadsden Purchase.

east   southwest   west

7. Canada is _____ of Mexico.

west   north   east

 **Think and Apply**

Cause and Effect   Match each cause on the left with an effect on the right. Write the letter of the effect on the correct blank.

Cause

1. In 1845 many Americans believed their country should be larger, so _____

2. Texas became a state, so _____

3. The United States captured Mexico City, so _____

4. In 1848 the United States got land in the Mexican Cession, so _____

5. Americans wanted to build a railroad across the southern part of the United States, so _____

Effect

a. they paid Mexico 10 million dollars for land in the Gadsden Purchase.

b. Mexico said there would be a war with the United States.

c. the country's borders went from the Atlantic Ocean to the Pacific Ocean.

d. the United States Congress voted for Texas to become a state.

e. Mexico surrendered.

Journal Writing

Mexicans who lived in the Southwest became American citizens after the Mexican War. Write a paragraph in your journal that tells how Mexican Americans helped the United States.

CHAPTER 19

ON TO OREGON AND CALIFORNIA

Think About As You Read

1. Why did people want to go to Oregon?
2. How did people travel to Oregon in the 1840s?
3. What happened after gold was found in California?

NEW WORDS

oxen
wagon train
Oregon Trail
coast
gold rush
pass

PEOPLE & PLACES

Oregon Country
Oregon
Independence, Missouri
Washington
Idaho
James Marshall
James Beckwourth
Beckwourth Pass

Families that traveled to Oregon crossed the Rocky Mountains in covered wagons.

Many Americans wanted to move west to Oregon Country in the 1840s. Oregon had lots of trees for building new houses. Oregon had good land for farming. Soon thousands of Americans moved west to build new homes and farms in Oregon Country.

The trip to Oregon Country was long and slow. There were no roads across the United States to Oregon. Families traveled to Oregon in covered wagons. Horses and **oxen** pulled the covered wagons. In 1843 many families in 120 covered wagons met in Independence, Missouri. These 120 covered wagons made a **wagon train**. The covered wagons traveled together across the Great Plains and the Rocky Mountains to Oregon. The trail they followed became known as the **Oregon Trail**.

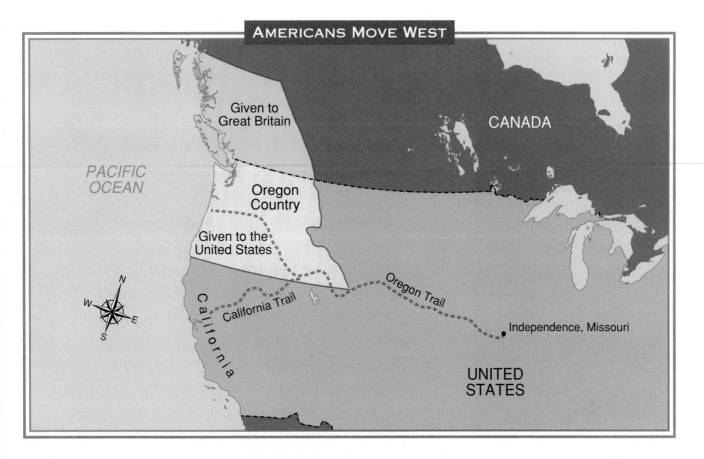

What was it like to travel on the Oregon Trail? Families woke up very early every day. Then people traveled as many hours as they could. At night they slept on the floors of their covered wagons. When it rained, wagon wheels got stuck in mud. Sometimes wagons turned over. Then people inside the wagons were hurt or killed. It was hard to find food on the way to Oregon. Many families were hungry. The wagons traveled across mountains, forests, and rivers. The long trip on the Oregon Trail took about six months.

At last the families reached Oregon Country. They had traveled 2,000 miles. Soon thousands of other people went to Oregon on the Oregon Trail. Each year more people settled along the Pacific **coast**.

Oregon Country was much bigger than our state of Oregon today. Oregon Country included part of Canada. Great Britain and the United States had shared Oregon Country for many years. The two nations could not decide on a way to divide Oregon. President Polk believed in Manifest Destiny. He wanted Oregon to be part of the

United States. Many people thought Great Britain and the United States would fight for Oregon. This time the two nations did not fight. The United States signed a treaty with Great Britain about Oregon in 1846.

The 1846 treaty said that the northern part of Oregon Country was part of Canada. Canada and northern Oregon belonged to Great Britain. Southern Oregon became part of the United States. Later the states of Oregon, Washington, and Idaho were made from the southern part of Oregon Country.

The United States government gave free farmland to families that moved to Oregon. Many Americans went to Oregon on the Oregon Trail for free land. In 1859 the United States Congress voted for Oregon to become a state.

While thousands of Americans were moving to the state of Oregon, other Americans were rushing to California. One day in 1848, a man named James Marshall found pieces of gold in a river in California. Soon everyone knew that James Marshall had found gold.

People from all over the United States began moving to California. They wanted to find gold and become rich.

Many people moved to California to look for gold.

James Beckwourth found a mountain pass that made it easier for Americans to travel west.

We say that California had a **gold rush** in 1848 and 1849 because thousands of people went to find gold.

The gold rush brought many kinds of people to California. Many people came from Europe to look for gold in California. People came from China to find gold. Free African Americans also moved to California.

James Beckwourth made it easier for many people to travel west to California. Beckwourth was an African American. He moved west and lived with American Indians. Tall mountains in the West made it hard to go to California. Beckwourth looked for an easier way to go across the mountains. At last Beckwourth found a **pass** through the mountains. Many people used this pass to reach California. Today that pass through the mountains is called the Beckwourth Pass.

Some people were lucky in California. They found gold and became rich. Most people did not find gold. Many people stayed in California. They built farms and factories. They started new cities. They built stores and houses. By 1850, 90,000 people were living in California. The United States Congress voted for California to become a state in 1850.

The California gold rush brought thousands of settlers to California. The Oregon Trail brought thousands of Americans to the Northwest. Every year more Americans moved west to California and Oregon.

Human/Environment Interaction: The Gold Rush

USING GEOGRAPHY THEMES

The theme of **human/environment interaction** tells how people live in an area. People in cold areas wear coats. People near oceans might fish for their food. The theme also tells how people can change an area. People use the land to help them live and work. They cut down trees to build houses and roads. They build canals so that ships can reach rivers or lakes.

Read the paragraphs about California's gold rush. Study the photo and the map.

Beginning in 1848, thousands of people rushed to California to search for gold. They started many mining camps. This gold rush changed California's land and rivers. The **environment** also changed how the **miners** lived.

When the gold rush began, people used their hands and tools to remove gold from rivers. Soon the gold in these rivers was gone. After 1850, miners began digging deep in the earth to find gold. Some miners built strong walls called **dams** to hold back the water in rivers. Then they dug deep into the ground where there had been water. Many miners dug tunnels to find gold. Others used huge amounts of water to break open mountain walls to find gold.

As the miners dug into the earth, dirt and rocks were dumped into rivers. The rivers became dirty. Most of the fish in the dirty rivers died.

The environment changed the lives of the miners. Miners spent most of their days searching for gold. At night, they often slept in tents on cold ground. When the fish died in the dirty rivers, miners had less food to eat. Sometimes the rivers spread lots of rocks over farmland. Farmers could not grow enough fruits and vegetables for miners to eat. Many miners became very sick because they did not eat well or sleep well.

Sutter Creek, California, was a mining town that began in 1848. The miners lived in tents. The town grew as more gold was found. The miners built houses. Today the gold is gone. Many people in Sutter Creek now sell wood from nearby forests to earn money.

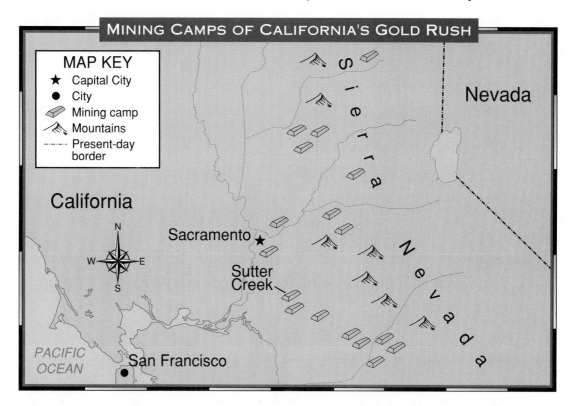

MINING CAMPS OF CALIFORNIA'S GOLD RUSH

MAP KEY
★ Capital City
● City
Mining camp
Mountains
Present-day border

Nevada

California

Sacramento ★

Sutter Creek

PACIFIC OCEAN

San Francisco

Sierra Nevada

On a separate sheet of paper, write the answer to each question.
1. Where did people look for gold at the start of California's gold rush?
2. What are three things the miners did to the earth in order to find gold?
3. Why did the fish die in many of California's rivers?
4. How did the lives of miners change when many fish were gone?
5. Why couldn't farmers grow enough crops for miners to eat?
6. How do many people in Sutter Creek earn money today?

Read and Remember ⭐

Finish the Sentence Draw a circle around the date, word, or words that finish each sentence.

1. Thousands of Americans went to Oregon Country in the _____ .
   1820s   1830s   1840s

2. In 1846 the northern part of Oregon Country became part of _____ .
   the United States   Canada   Washington

3. Families that moved to Oregon were given free _____ .
   wagons   houses   farmland

4. In 1848 and 1849, Americans rushed to California to find _____ .
   silver   gold   trees

5. California became a state in _____ .
   1850   1859   1860

6. The Oregon Trail began in _____ .
   Philadelphia   New Orleans   Independence

⭐ Think and Apply

Categories Read the words in each group. Decide how they are alike. Find the best title in blue print for each group. Write the title on the line above each group.

James Beckwourth   California   Oregon Trail   Gold Rush

1. _____
   1848 and 1849
   search for gold
   brought thousands to California

2. _____
   African American
   lived in the West
   found a pass through the mountains

3. _____
   horses and oxen
   covered wagons
   went to Oregon

4. _____
   gold rush
   new cities
   90,000 people in 1850

Skill Builder

Reading a Historical Map   The map below shows how the United States became a large country. Study each area and when it became part of the United States.

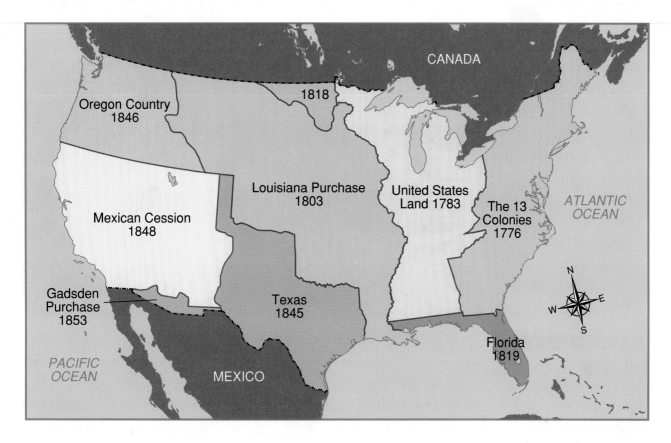

Draw a circle around the correct answer.

1. What land made up the United States in 1776?
   Texas   the 13 Colonies   Louisiana

2. What southeast land belonged to Spain until 1819?
   Oregon Country   Texas   Florida

3. What land did the United States get in 1848?
   Mexican Cession   Louisiana Purchase   Texas

4. Which northwest land became part of the United States in 1846?
   Oregon Country   Florida   Louisiana Purchase

5. Which land did the United States buy in 1853?
   Gadsden Purchase   Oregon Country   Texas

CHAPTER 20

THE SOUTHERN STATES LEAVE

Think About As You Read

1. **Why were there more slaves in the South than in the North?**
2. **Why did the South become angry with the North?**
3. **What did the South do after Abraham Lincoln became President?**

NEW WORDS

quarreling
plantations
sugar cane
escape
Fugitive Slave Act
Union

PEOPLE & PLACES

Harriet Tubman
Abraham Lincoln
Confederate States of America
Jefferson Davis

On plantations in the South, slaves did most of the farm work.

The United States had become a large country after the Mexican War. But things were not going well in the United States. The northern states were **quarreling** with the southern states. The northern states were called the North, and the southern states were called the South. Why did the North and South quarrel?

An important problem was slavery. In the early days of our nation, there were slaves both in the North and in the South. But farms were small in the North. The North had many factories. Most people there did not need slaves to work on their farms and in factories. There were fewer slaves in the North.

In the South some people owned very large farms called **plantations**. The owners grew cotton, **sugar cane**, and tobacco on their plantations. Plantation owners needed many workers. Many plantation owners bought slaves to do the work. The plantation owners thought they could not grow crops without slaves.

A small group of rich plantation owners owned most of the slaves. Most people in the South did not own any slaves. But almost everyone in the South agreed that slavery should be allowed. The North did not agree.

After the Mexican War, more Americans moved to the West. People from the South started new plantations in the West. They wanted to bring their slaves. The northern states did not want slavery in the West.

The North and South began to quarrel. In the North many people said that all people should be free. They said that it was not right for one person to own another person. In the South people said that the Constitution allowed slavery. People in the South said that people in the North should not tell them what to do. The people in the North wanted to make new laws against slavery in the West. This made the South very angry.

Plantation owners in the South bought and sold slaves.

Many slaves escaped to the North.

Harriet Tubman

The South was worried because many Americans had become abolitionists. They were working to end slavery. Some people wrote books and newspapers that told why slavery was wrong. Some people gave speeches against slavery. Other people helped slaves run away from their owners.

Harriet Tubman was one of the people who helped slaves become free. Harriet Tubman had been a slave herself. She had run away to the North. In the North she became a free woman. She went back to the South and helped slaves **escape** to Canada. In Canada the slaves were free. Harriet Tubman helped hundreds of slaves get their freedom.

In 1850 Congress passed a law about slaves who escaped to the North. It was called the **Fugitive Slave Act**. The new law said that all escaped slaves must be returned to the South. People who did not return slaves were punished. This new law made the North very angry with the South.

In 1861 a man named Abraham Lincoln became the President of the United States. What kind of man was Abraham Lincoln? He came from a poor family. He lived very far from school when he was young. He only went to school for about one year. Lincoln learned as much as he could by reading books. He grew up to be very tall, thin,

Abraham Lincoln came from a poor family.

Abraham Lincoln

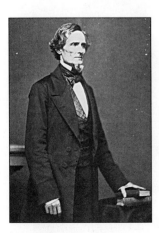

Jefferson Davis

and strong. He became a lawyer. Many people liked Lincoln because he was honest and smart.

President Lincoln believed that slavery was wrong. He promised he would not try to end slavery in the South. But he said slavery should not be allowed in the West. The North liked what Lincoln said, but the South did not. The South believed Lincoln would work to end slavery everywhere.

Seven southern states decided they no longer wanted to be part of the **Union**. The Union is another name for the United States. In 1861 these seven southern states started a new country. They called their country the Confederate States of America. The Confederate States wrote their own constitution. It had laws that allowed slavery. The Confederate States had their own flag and their own money. Jefferson Davis became the president of the Confederate States. Soon four other southern states joined the Confederate States.

President Lincoln said that the United States must be one country, not two. Would the Union and the Confederate States become one country again? Would it take a war to bring them together? Read Chapter 21 to find the answers to these questions.

USING GEOGRAPHY THEMES

The theme of **region** tells how places in an area are alike. A region can be large or small. Places in a region might have the same weather or kind of land. People in a region might share customs, ideas, and ways of life.

Read the paragraphs about the South in 1861. Study the photo and the map.

The South was a region with huge plantations. Plantations were the center of southern life. The South was a good place for farms and plantations. There was plenty of good soil. There were rain and a warm **climate** during most of the year. Plantation owners grew crops such as cotton, sugar cane, tobacco, and rice. Cotton was the most important crop. The South earned most of its money by selling its cotton.

Slaves did most of the farm work on the plantations. Plantation owners believed they could not grow cotton and other crops without the work of slaves. By 1861 one third of the people in the South were African American slaves.

The South was very different from the North. It did not have many big cities, factories, and railroads like the North. New Orleans was the biggest city in the South. But it was smaller than many cities in the North.

While many people in the North were moving to cities, most people in the South worked at farming. Many people owned small farms. Most of the farmers did not own slaves. But almost everyone in the South agreed that the region needed slavery.

In 1861 most people in the South said they would fight to keep their slaves and their way of life. Seven southern states decided to leave the United States. They did not want to be part of a country that might end slavery. They started a new country called the Confederate States of America. Later four other states joined the Confederate States.

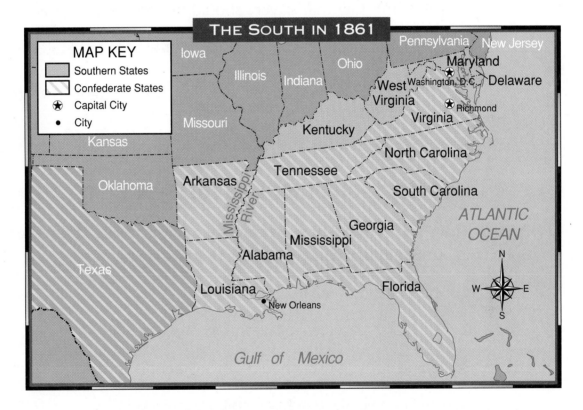

On a separate sheet of paper, write the answer to each question.

1. Why was the South a good place for farms and plantations?
2. What was the most important crop in the South?
3. How was the South different from the North?
4. Why did some southern states start a new country?
5. Look at the map. Which four southern states did **not** join the Confederate States of America?

⭐ Read and Remember

True or False Write **T** next to each sentence that is true. Write **F** next to each sentence that is false.

_____ 1. The North had small farms and many factories.

_____ 2. People grew cotton, sugar cane, and tobacco in the South.

_____ 3. Slaves worked on many large plantations in the North.

_____ 4. Harriet Tubman only helped three slaves escape.

_____ 5. The North said that slavery should be allowed in the West.

_____ 6. Abraham Lincoln became President of the United States in 1861.

_____ 7. Thirteen northern states left the United States and became the Confederate States of America.

_____ 8. The Confederate States had their own constitution, flag, and money.

Think and Apply ⭐

Fact or Opinion Write **F** next to each fact below. Write **O** next to each opinion. You should find four sentences that are opinions.

_____ 1. The Constitution allowed slavery.

_____ 2. The North had fewer slaves than the South did.

_____ 3. People in the North should not tell people in the South what to do.

_____ 4. The Fugitive Slave Act was not a good law.

_____ 5. Jefferson Davis became president of the Confederate States.

_____ 6. President Lincoln did not want slavery in the West.

_____ 7. People in the South were the best farmers.

_____ 8. Abolitionists were working to end slavery.

_____ 9. The southern states were wrong to leave the Union.

Skill Builder

Reading a Bar Graph Graphs are drawings that help you compare facts. The graph on this page is a **bar graph**. It shows facts using bars of different lengths. The bar graph below shows the number of people who lived in the United States in 1860. Study the bar graph.

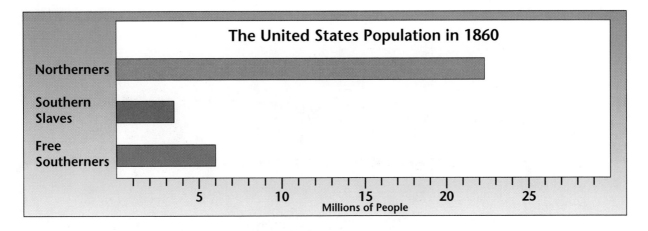

The United States Population in 1860

Draw a circle around the correct answer.

1. About how many people lived in the North?
   $3\frac{1}{2}$ million   6 million   22 million

2. About how many slaves lived in the South?
   $3\frac{1}{2}$ million   6 million   22 million

3. Which group had the largest population?
   Northerners   Free Southerners   Southern Slaves

4. Which group had about 6 million people?
   Northerners   Free Southerners   Southern Slaves

5. What was the total number of people living in the South?
   $3\frac{1}{2}$ million $9\frac{1}{2}$ million   16 million

 Journal Writing

Harriet Tubman helped slaves escape. Why did she help them? Write a paragraph in your journal that tells why Tubman helped slaves.

THE CIVIL WAR

Think About As You Read

1. What did the South fight for during the Civil War?
2. What did the North fight for during the Civil War?
3. Why did Robert E. Lee surrender?

NEW WORDS

Civil War
goal
Emancipation
  Proclamation
battlefields
destroyed
rebuild

PEOPLE & PLACES

Fort Sumter
Confederates
Robert E. Lee
Clara Barton
Ulysses S. Grant
Richmond

Many soldiers from both the North and the South died in the Civil War.

The South had started a new country called the Confederate States of America. President Lincoln did not want the North to fight against the South. He wanted the South to become part of the United States again. The South also did not want a war. But the South did not want to be part of the Union.

The United States Army owned a fort called Fort Sumter in South Carolina. South Carolina was one of the Confederate States. People who lived in the Confederate States were called Confederates. They said that the United States must give Fort Sumter to the Confederate States of America. But Union soldiers would not surrender Fort Sumter.

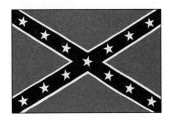

Confederate battle flag

In 1861 Confederate soldiers began to shoot at Fort Sumter. A war between the North and South had begun. This war was called the **Civil War**. The Civil War lasted four years. People in the South fought to have their own country, the Confederate States of America. The North fought so that all states would remain in the Union.

The Confederates thought they would win. They had many good army generals and brave soldiers. But the North was stronger than the South. The North had more people and more soldiers. The North had more money to pay for a war. The North had more railroads. Union soldiers traveled on these railroads to many places. The North had more factories, too. Northern factories made guns for the war. The South had few factories.

Robert E. Lee was the leader of the Confederate army. Lee loved the United States. He did not like slavery. He also loved his own state of Virginia. President Lincoln wanted Robert E. Lee to lead the Union army. But Lee would not fight against his family and friends in Virginia. Instead, he became the leader

Robert E. Lee

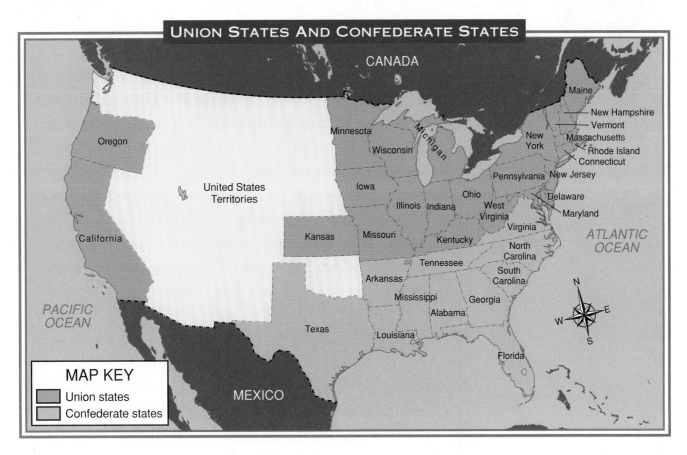

UNION STATES AND CONFEDERATE STATES

CANADA

Maine

New Hampshire

Vermont

Minnesota

Wisconsin

Michigan

New York

Massachusetts

Rhode Island

Connecticut

Oregon

Pennsylvania New Jersey

Iowa

Ohio

Delaware

United States Territories

Illinois Indiana

West Virginia

Maryland

Virginia

California

Kansas

Missouri

Kentucky

ATLANTIC OCEAN

North Carolina

Tennessee

Arkansas

South Carolina

Mississippi

Georgia

PACIFIC OCEAN

Alabama

Texas

Louisiana

N

Florida

W E

S

MAP KEY

Union states

Confederate states

MEXICO

Many African Americans joined the Union army and fought in the Civil War.

Clara Barton

Major Civil War battles

of the Confederate army. General Lee was a good leader. He led the Confederate army for four long years.

President Lincoln had a **goal**. His goal was for the North and South to be one nation. He decided to help the Union win by working to end slavery. In 1862 he wrote a paper that said all slaves in the Confederate States were free. He wrote that the slaves would be free on January 1, 1863. The paper was called the **Emancipation Proclamation**. Many African American slaves left the South. Thousands of brave African Americans joined the Union army. They fought in many battles of the Civil War.

Women in the North and South helped during the war. They managed farms and factories. Some women became spies. Many women became nurses. Clara Barton was a famous Union nurse. She traveled to many **battlefields**. Clara Barton cared for soldiers who were hurt.

At the start of the Civil War, the South won many battles. After two years the South lost more and more battles. Most of the Civil War battles were fought in the South. The fighting **destroyed** houses, cities, and plantations in the South.

General Ulysses S. Grant was the leader of the Union army. He won many battles. In 1865 the Union soldiers captured

President Abraham Lincoln was shot soon after the end of the Civil War.

Ulysses S. Grant

Richmond, Virginia. Richmond was the capital of the Confederate States. General Lee knew the Confederates could not win the war. There was very little food to eat in the South. Lee's army was hungry. The soldiers did not have enough guns. Lee did not want more people to die in the war. Lee surrendered to Grant in April 1865. The Civil War was over. Plans were made to return the Confederate States to the Union. General Lee returned to Virginia. He told the South to help the United States become a strong country.

President Lincoln was glad that the United States was one nation again. He was also unhappy. Almost 600,000 soldiers in the North and South had been killed. Thousands of other soldiers were badly hurt.

President Lincoln had new goals when the war ended. He wanted Americans to work together to **rebuild** the South. Lincoln wanted Americans in the North and South to like one another again.

President Lincoln never reached these goals. He was shot five days after the Civil War ended. President Lincoln died the next day. Americans in the North and South were sad because a great leader was dead.

People in the North and the South were united once again. It would take many more years to end the anger between the North and the South. But together they would continue to make the United States a great nation.

Read and Remember

Write the Answer   Write a sentence to answer each question.

1. What did the North fight for in the Civil War? _____

   _____

2. What did the South fight for in the Civil War? _____

   _____

3. What was the Emancipation Proclamation? _____

   _____

4. How did women help during the Civil War? _____

   _____

5. What was one reason General Lee surrendered to General Grant? _____

   _____

Think and Apply

Sequencing Events   Write the numbers **1**, **2**, **3**, **4**, and **5** next to these sentences to show the correct order.

_____ In 1862 President Lincoln wrote the Emancipation Proclamation.

_____ In 1861 Confederate soldiers attacked Fort Sumter.

_____ President Lincoln was killed after the war ended.

_____ The war ended when General Robert E. Lee surrendered to General Ulysses S. Grant.

_____ In 1865 the Union captured the Confederate capital at Richmond, Virginia.

Journal Writing

The Civil War was a long, hard war between the Union and the Confederate States. Write a paragraph about the Civil War in your journal. Tell how it began or how it ended. Write at least five sentences.

Skill Builder

Reading a Table   A **table** lists a group of facts. You can compare facts by reading a table. Look at the table below. It compares the North and South before the Civil War. To learn facts about the North and the South, read the numbers listed beneath each heading. Read the table from left to right to find out what the numbers in the table stand for.

The North and South Before the Civil War		
	North	South
Money	$330,000,000	$47,000,000
Number of factories and shops	111,000	21,000
Miles of railroad track	22,000	9,000
Horses	3,400,000	1,700,000
Units of wheat	132,000,000	31,000

Draw a circle around the number, word, or words that finish each sentence.

1. The South had _____ miles of railroad track before the Civil War.
   22,000   9,000   111,000

2. The North had _____ factories and shops before the war.
   3,400,000   21,000   111,000

3. The South had _____ money than the North did before the war.
   more   less   the same amount of

4. The North had _____ horses than the South did.
   more   fewer   the same number of

5. The North had _____ units of wheat for food than the South did.
   more   fewer   the same number of

6. Based on the chart, the North was _____ the South was.
   stronger than   weaker than   about the same as

Study the time line on this page. Then use the words in blue print to finish the story. Write the words you choose on the correct blank lines.

slaves	Lincoln	state
Texas	California	Lee
Cession	Confederate	Civil War

In 1836 _____ won a war for independence from Mexico.

In 1845 Texas became a _____ . The United States fought

a war with Mexico. From that war the United States got the Mexican

_____ . Many Americans moved west. After the gold rush,

_____ became a state in 1850.

As the nation grew larger, the North and the South quarreled about slavery.

In 1861 southern states started a new nation called the _____

States of America. Later that year, the _____ began. President

Abraham Lincoln wrote the Emancipation Proclamation. This paper said that

_____ in the Confederate States were free. In 1865 General

_____ surrendered to General Grant. The Union had won the

Civil War. A few days later, _____ was killed.

			1861	1865
			The southern	General Lee
1836		1850	states start	surrenders to
Texas wins	1845	California	the Confederate	General Grant.
independence	Texas becomes	becomes	States of	The Civil War is
from Mexico.	a state.	a state.	America. The	over. Abraham
			Civil War begins.	Lincoln is killed.

| 1830 | 1840 | 1850 | 1860 | 1870 |

	1848	1859	1863
	The United	Oregon	President
	States gets	becomes	Lincoln
	the Mexican	a state.	frees the
	Cession.		slaves in the
			Confederate
			States.

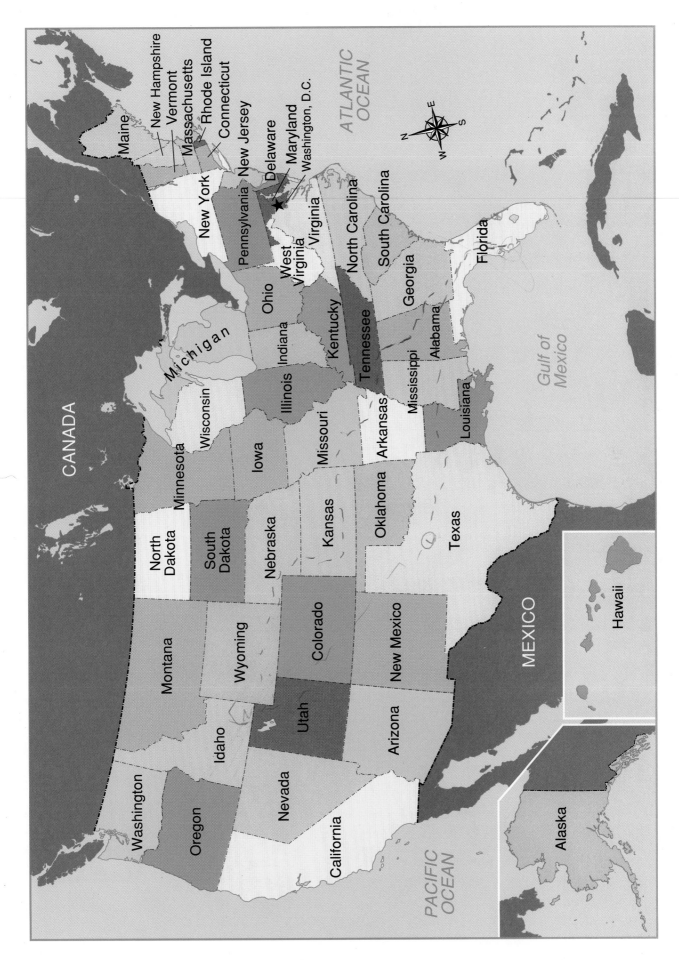

CANADA

Maine
New Hampshire
Vermont
Massachusetts
Rhode Island
Connecticut
New York
New Jersey
Delaware
Maryland
Washington, D.C.
Pennsylvania
West Virginia
Virginia
North Carolina
South Carolina
Ohio
Kentucky
Tennessee
Georgia
Michigan
Indiana
Alabama
Wisconsin
Illinois
Missouri
Mississippi
Louisiana
Arkansas
Minnesota
Iowa
Kansas
Oklahoma
Texas
North Dakota
South Dakota
Nebraska
Colorado
New Mexico
Montana
Wyoming
Utah
Arizona
Idaho
Nevada
California
Washington
Oregon

ATLANTIC OCEAN
Florida
Gulf of Mexico
MEXICO
Hawaii
Alaska
PACIFIC OCEAN

N
E
S
W

145

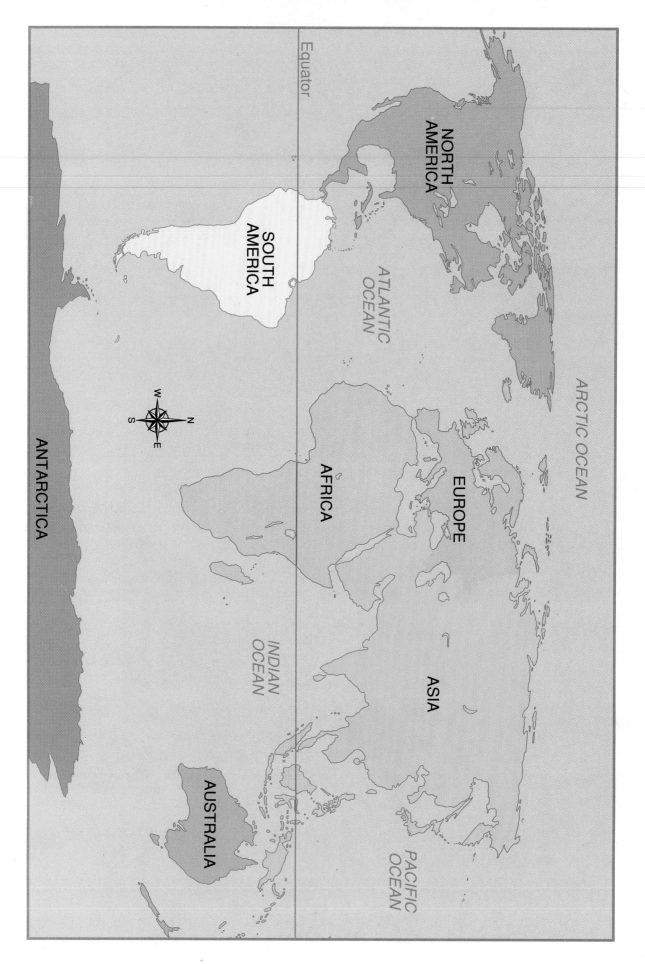

abolitionists page 103
Abolitionists were people who worked to end slavery in the United States.

amendments page 68
Amendments are laws that are added to the Constitution.

American Revolution page 43
The American Revolution was the war that the American colonies fought against Great Britain from 1775 to 1781.

assured page 50
Assured means made sure or certain.

battlefields page 140
Battlefields are areas of land on which battles are fought.

Bill of Rights page 68
The Bill of Rights is the first ten amendments added to the Constitution.

body of water page 32
A body of water is a large area of water. Lakes, rivers, and oceans are bodies of water.

border page 93
A border is a line that separates one state from another. A border can also separate cities, towns, and countries.

Boston Tea Party page 42
During the Boston Tea Party, Americans went on three British tea ships. They threw all the tea into the ocean because they did not want to pay a tea tax.

boundaries page 61
Boundaries are the lines around a city, state, or country. Rivers, oceans, and mountains can be boundaries. Boundaries are often shown as lines drawn on maps.

branches of government page 67
The three branches of government in the United States are Congress, the President, and the Supreme Court, as well as the people who work for them.

buffalo page 5
Buffalo are oxen. They are large animals with horns and fur.

canals page 90
Canals are waterways that connect bodies of water, such as rivers.

capital page 17
The capital of a country or a state is the city where the government meets.

captured page 80
Captured means took and held a person, place, or thing by using force.

Church of England page 20
The Church of England is all the churches in England that accept the ruler of England as the head of the church.

citizens page 118
Citizens are members of a country.

Civil War page 139
The Civil War was the war fought between the North and the South from 1861 and 1865.

claimed page 11
When a country claimed land, it meant it would own and rule that land.

climate page 134
Climate is the usual weather in an area.

coast page 123
A coast is land along an ocean.

colony page 25
A colony is land ruled by another nation.

commander in chief page 59
The commander in chief is the most important leader of the American army.

Congress page 66
Congress is the United States Senate and House of Representatives. Men and women in Congress write laws for the United States.

Constitution page 55
A constitution is a set of laws. The United States Constitution is a set of laws for the United States.

Constitutional Convention page 60
The Constitutional Convention was a set of important meetings in 1787. During the meetings, American leaders wrote a set of new laws for the United States.

cotton page 5
Cotton is a plant used to make cloth. You can wear clothes made of cotton.

cotton gin page 88
A cotton gin is a machine that removes seeds from cotton plants.

crops page 75
Crops are plants grown by farmers. Corn, potatoes, and cotton are three kinds of crops.

dams page 126
Dams are strong walls built to hold back water in rivers.

Declaration of Independence page 46
The Declaration of Independence was an important paper that said the American colonies were a free nation.

destroyed page 140
Destroyed means ruined. A war can destroy homes, farms, and cities.

disabilities page 103
People with disabilities are less able to do certain things. Not being able to hear or see is a disability.

doubled page 76
When the United States doubled in size, it became twice as large as it had been.

education page 102
Education is the learning a person gets from school, people, and places.

electric sparks page 54
Electric sparks are tiny bits of electricity that give off small amounts of light for a few seconds.

Emancipation Proclamation page 140
The Emancipation Proclamation was a paper that said all slaves in the Confederate States were free. It went into effect in 1863.

environment page 126
The environment is the land, water, and climate of an area.

equal page 46
People who are equal have the same importance.

escape page 132
To escape means to get free.

First Lady page 61
The wife of the President of the United States is called the First Lady.

fort page 112
A fort is a building from which an army can fight its enemies.

freedom of religion page 20
Freedom of religion means one can pray the way he or she wants to pray.

freedom of the press page 68
Freedom of the press means a person can write what he or she wants to write in newspapers and books.

freedom of the seas page 80
Freedom of the seas means that people can sail ships wherever they want.

Fugitive Slave Act page 132
The Fugitive Slave Act was a law passed in 1850. It said that all escaped slaves must be returned to the South.

Gadsden Purchase page 118
The Gadsden Purchase was land that the United States bought from Mexico.

general page 47
A general is an important army leader.

geographers page 17
Geographers are people who study different areas and people on Earth.

goal page 140
A goal is something a person wants and tries to get.

gold rush page 125
A gold rush is a time when many people move into an area in order to find gold.

goods page 87
Goods are things people buy.

governor page 21
A governor is a government leader for a state, town, or area.

Great Spirit page 84
Many American Indians believe in the Great Spirit, their most important god. They believe the Great Spirit made them and placed them on the land.

House of Representatives page 66
The House of Representatives is one of the two houses, or parts, of Congress. It has 435 members.

human/environment interaction page 126
The geography theme of human/environment interaction tells how people can change an area. It also tells how people live in an area.

in debt page 27
A person who is in debt owes money to other people.

independent page 46
Independent means free. An independent country rules itself.

Industrial Revolution page 87
The Industrial Revolution was a change from making goods by hand to making goods by machine.

invented page 87
Invented means thought up or made for the first time.

justices page 67
Justices are judges. There are nine justices in the Supreme Court.

lame page 50
Lame means hurt. If a person's feet or legs are lame, it is hard for that person to walk.

location page 62
The geography theme of location tells where a place is found.

locomotives page 90
Locomotives are engines used to pull trains.

Louisiana Purchase page 76
The Louisiana Purchase was the sale of a large piece of land west of the Mississippi River. The United States bought it from France in 1803.

Loyalists page 47
Loyalists were Americans who did not want the 13 colonies to become independent. Loyalists helped Great Britain during the American Revolution.

manage page 58
To manage means to control and take care of something.

Manifest Destiny page 116
Manifest Destiny was the idea that the United States should rule land from the Atlantic Ocean to the Pacific Ocean.

mass production page 88
In mass production, people or machines make many goods that are exactly alike.

Mayflower Compact page 21
The Mayflower Compact was the Pilgrims' plan for ruling themselves in America.

mental illness page 103
People with mental illness have a disease or condition that changes the way they think.

Mexican Cession page 118
The Mexican Cession was land that the United States got as a result of the Mexican War.

miners page 126
Miners are people who dig in the earth to find gold or other metals or stones.

miserable page 84
To be miserable is to be unhappy.

missions page 16
Missions are places where people teach others how to become Christians.

movement page 97
The geography theme of movement tells how people, goods, and ideas move from one place to another.

nation page 40
A nation is a large group of people living together in one country.

navy page 81
The navy is a nation's warships and all the people who work on the warships.

New World page 11
People in Europe called North America and South America the New World because they had not known about these continents.

Oregon Trail page 122
The Oregon Trail was the trail that wagons followed through the West to Oregon.

oxen page 122
An ox is an animal like a cow. Oxen is the word used for more than one ox.

Parliament page 41
The people who write laws for Great Britain are called Parliament. They work in the Parliament Building.

pass page 125
A pass is a trail through mountains.

peace treaty page 22
A peace treaty is an agreement not to fight.

peril page 114
To peril means to put in danger.

place page 17
The geography theme of place tells what makes an area different from other areas in the world.

plantations page 130
Plantations are very large farms where crops such as cotton and sugar cane are grown.

port page 42
A port is a place by an ocean or river where ships are loaded and unloaded.

priests page 16
Priests are people who lead religious services and teach about the Catholic religion.

primary sources page 28
Primary sources are the words and objects of people who have lived at different times. Some primary sources are journals, letters, and tools.

printer page 53
A printer is a person who prints books and newspapers.

printing shop page 53
A printing shop is a place with machines for printing books and newspapers.

promptly page 114
Promptly means soon.

property page 119
All the land and other things a person owns are his or her property.

provisions page 114
Provisions are food and other supplies.

published page 53
Published means prepared a book or newspaper so it could be sold.

quarreling page 130
Quarreling means arguing or not agreeing about something.

race page 84
A race is a group of people sharing the same beginnings from long ago. They usually have similar eyes and skin color.

rebuild page 141
To rebuild means to build something again.

recovered page 50
Recovered means got better.

reform page 101
Reform is a change to make something, such as a school or government, better.

region page 134
The geography theme of region tells how places in an area are alike.

relief page 114
Relief is help from others.

religions page 4
Religions are the ways people believe in and pray to a god or to many gods.

religious page 26
Religious means having to do with religion.

representatives page 66
People who make laws in the House of Representatives are called representatives.

republic page 113
A republic is a country where people vote for their leaders. These leaders make laws for the people and lead the government.

Senate page 66
The Senate is one of the two houses, or parts, of Congress. It has 100 members.

senators page 66
People who make laws in the Senate are senators.

settlers page 25
Settlers are people who go to live in a new place.

short cut page 31
A short cut is a shorter way to go to a place.

slavery page 16
Slavery is the owning of people, or slaves. Slaves are forced to work without pay.

snowshoes page 33
Snowshoes are wooden frames that a person can attach to shoes to help him or her walk on deep snow.

spices page 9
Spices are added to food to improve the way it tastes and smells.

Stamp Act page 41
The Stamp Act said that Americans in the British colonies had to pay a tax on things made from paper.

steamboat page 89
A steamboat is a boat that is powered by a steam engine.

steam engine page 89
A steam engine is a machine that uses steam to create power for other machines.

sugar cane page 130
People get sugar from the tall plant called sugar cane.

Supreme Court page 67
The Supreme Court is the highest court in the United States. It decides whether laws agree with the Constitution.

surrendered page 59
An army that surrendered in a war stopped fighting and agreed that it lost.

tariffs page 96
Tariffs are taxes on goods from other countries.

tax page 41
Tax is money that a person must pay to the government.

Texas Revolution page 113
The Texas Revolution was the war that Texans fought in order to win their independence from Mexico.

themes page 17
Themes are main ideas. The five themes of geography help geographers learn about areas and people on Earth.

tobacco page 26
Tobacco is a plant. The leaves of this plant are smoked in pipes, cigars, and cigarettes.

Trail of Tears page 96
When the Cherokee were forced to move west to Indian Territory, they called their trip the Trail of Tears.

troops page 50
Troops are soldiers in an army.

Union page 133
The Union is the United States.

unite page 84
To unite is to join together.

victory page 114
A victory is a win.

wagon train page 122
Covered wagons that traveled together on a trail formed a wagon train.

INDEX